WRITERS AND CRITICS

Chief Editor
A. NORMAN JEFFARES

Advisory Editors
DAVID DAICHES

C. P. SNOW

In this book Professor Humphreys relates Melville's writing to his wide reading, and to his variety of interests and experience. He explains Melville's more complex works as straightforwardly as possible, and treats the novels not as moral or symbolical puzzles but as documents related directly to the problems of living.

Melville's imaginative daring, his adventurous thinking, his wonderful if erratically gifted writing, led him to explore modes and values of human existence. *Moby Dick*, for instance, displays a complex allegory of life in the guise of a whaling adventure. Professor Humphreys, regarding this as Melville's supreme achievement, devotes a third of this book to it.

The author's interest in American literature dates from two years spent in Harvard after graduating from Cambridge, where he was a member of St Catharine's College. He has taught at the Universities of Cambridge, Liverpool, and Istanbul (where he was on secondment from the R.A.F.). Since 1947 he has been Professor of English at the University of Leicester.

MELVILLE

A. R. HUMPHREYS

NEW YORK

BARNES & NOBLE, INC.

Publishers · Booksellers · Since 1873

OLIVER AND BOYD LTD
Tweeddale Court
Edinburgh 1

39A Welbeck Street
London W.1

Published in the United States
in 1966
by Barnes & Noble Inc.
New York, N.Y.

Printed in Great Britain
by Robert MacLehose and Co. Ltd, Glasgow

CONTENTS

ACKNOWLEDGMENTS

Acknowledgments are due to the following publishers for permission to quote from the works indicated:

Edward Arnold Ltd and Harcourt, Brace and World, Inc. (E. M. Forster, *Aspects of the Novel*); Columbia University Press (Charles R. Anderson, *Melville in the South Seas*); Harcourt, Brace and World, Inc. and Jonathan Cape Ltd (Lewis Mumford, *Herman Melville*); Harvard University Press (E. M. Metcalf, *Herman Melville: Cycle and Epicycle*); William Morrow and Co., Inc. (Yvor Winters, *In Defense of Reason*); Princeton University Press and Oxford University Press (Herman Melville, *Journal of a Visit to Europe and the Levant 1856-7*, ed. Howard C. Horsford); Yale University Press (*Letters of Herman Melville*, edd. Merrell R. Davis and William H. Gilman).

The portrait by Joseph Oriel Eaton has been reproduced on the front cover by kind permission of the Houghton Library of Harvard University and Mrs Henry K. Metcalf.

Finally, it is a pleasure to acknowledge how willingly aid was given by the United States Information Service and its Library at the American Embassy in London, in particular by Dr. Everett Gleason the Cultural Attaché and Miss Margaret Haferd the Librarian, and to express gratitude to Mr Charles E. Pettee for information supplied, and to Mr R. L. C. Lorimer, Oliver and Boyd Ltd, for the editorial skill and interest he has shown at all stages.

A.R.H.

For

JOHN *and* EDWINA

ABBREVIATED TITLES
BY WHICH MELVILLE'S WORKS
ARE CITED IN REFERENCES

C.M.	=	*The Confidence-Man.*
I.P.	=	*Israel Potter.*
J. 1849	=	*Journal of a Visit to London and the Continent, 1849–1850,* ed. Eleanor Melville Metcalf, 1948.
J. 1856	=	*Journal of a Visit to Europe and the Levant, October 11, 1856–May 6, 1857,* ed. Howard C. Horsford, 1955.
M.	=	*Mardi; and a Voyage Thither.*
M.D.	=	*Moby Dick.*
O.	=	*Omoo.*
P.	=	*Pierre: or, The Ambiguities.*
P.T.	=	*The Piazza Tales.*
R.	=	*Redburn.*
st. ed.	=	Standard Edition of the *Works of Herman Melville,* 16 vols., London (Constable) 1922–4.
T.	=	*Typee.*
W.J.	=	*White Jacket.*

For refs. to *M., M.D.,* and *P.,* see below, first section of Bibliography, p. 115.

OTHER ABBREVIATED TITLES

Leyda	=	*The Melville Log,* ed. Jay Leyda, 2 vols., 1951.
Metcalf	=	Eleanor Melville Metcalf, *Herman Melville, Cycle and Epicycle,* 1953.

CHAPTER I

LIFE

Providing "the plain man's guide" to Ezra Pound,[1] G. S. Fraser called his subject "the most morally, aesthetically, and culturally controversial literary figure of this century." Herman Melville might claim a like eminence in the nineteenth century, since his attitudes to life and his modes of writing are Protean in variety. In no writer are exceptional powers and weaknesses more intimately interlaced, and none has provoked more varied interpretations. As well as being a great novelist he was an extremely original one, and in his most ambitious works was pressed by intense compulsions into modes of exploration and expression both unpredictable and ambiguous. The following account will be as plain as I can make it, though no-one not a superlative critic could hope entirely to avoid complication and even confusion. Space, unfortunately, allows no examination of the poems; the stories alone offer all too much for a brief commentary.

Born in New York on 1 August 1819, Melville descended on his father's side from an eighteenth-century Scots immigrant, on his mother's from the earliest Dutch stock in America. His father, Allan Melville (1782–1832), traded in New York, travelled extensively to Europe, and felt a pride of ancestry which made him compile a genealogy stretching back to the thirteenth century. This pride Herman Melville shared; one of the first things that Sophia Hawthorne learnt when she first met him in 1850 was that "He is of Scotch descent—of noble lineage —of the Lords of Melville & Leven."[2] Though politically democratic (often sardonically so) Melville was a natural aristocrat in his sense of personal merit and quality, and comes himself to the reader's mind when in *Billy Budd* he writes of "the modesty of manhood sometimes accompanying a resolute nature, . . . which shown in any rank suggests a virtue aristocratic in kind". His mother's forebears were prosperous Dutch-Colonial merchants and industrialists; the most distinguished, eulogized in *Pierre*, was his grandfather Peter Gansevoort, a leading general of the War of Independence, one of whose sons, another Peter, was later to pay for the publication of Melville's poem *Clarel*.

His father went bankrupt in 1830 and died in 1832. Melville finished his schooling, clerked in his brother's store, schoolmastered briefly, and then in 1839 shipped as a deck-hand on the *St Lawrence*, a packet-ship which made the trip to Liverpool recorded in *Redburn*. In 1840, seeking employment, he visited an uncle in Galena, Illinois, but Galena offered no work, and he made that Mississippi journey thence to Cairo at the confluence of the Ohio, which he was to reorganise in *The Confidence-Man*, reaching New York in November. Next month he was at New Bedford, the whaling port south of Cape Cod, and on 31 December 1840, at the adjoining port of Fairhaven, he signed on the whaler *Acushnet*—"my Yale College and my Harvard."[3]

The *Acushnet* was new; her owners apparently knew the Melvilles; its men were mostly New-Englanders; and it carried a library. However, Melville deserted in the Marquesas in July 1842 with a companion, Richard Tobias Greene, the Toby of *Typee*. The voyage clearly was not all "the many pleasant moonlight watches we passed together on the deck of the 'Acushnet' as we whiled away the hours with yarn and song" that Toby recalled in 1861.[4] Indeed, in 1850 Melville heard from an old shipmate the fates of the *Acushnet*'s crew, a grim story of fighting, desertion, suicide, and disease, venereal and other. Four weeks after deserting (not the "four months" of *Typee*) he was taken off by the *Lucy Ann* (the *Julia* of *Typee* and *Omoo*), an Australian barque which reached Tahiti with its crew mutinous. *Omoo* amusingly describes their farcical imprisonment in an open-air calaboose. In November 1842, he shipped on his third whaler, the *Charles and Henry*, of Nantucket. He was discharged in the Hawaiian Islands in May 1843; and having had a spell ashore as store-keeper he signed as an ordinary seaman on the American frigate *United States*. In August there began that return voyage which, with much creative alteration, is magnificently related in *White Jacket*, and which took him, in the late summer of 1844, round the Horn, and so to Boston, where his deckhand life ended.

Early in 1845 he began *Typee*, and his brother Gansevoort, Secretary of the American Legation in London, showed it to John Murray, who published it in 1846. A New York edition soon followed. The general reception was encouraging, and with prospects of a literary career Melville married Elizabeth, daughter of Lemuel Shaw, the Chief Justice of Massachusetts, and settled in New York. *Omoo* appeared early in 1847 and was a successful sequel to *Typee*; and then he began what his literary sponsor Evert Duyckinck described to his brother George as "a third book which will exhaust the South-Sea marvels." This, however, under its author's experimental temper and the miscellaneous reading he was pursuing in New York, turned into the moral-satirical fantasy of *Mardi* (1849). From his earliest publication, "Fragments from a Writing-Desk" in the *Lansingburgh Advertiser* in 1839, he had compounded his reading into his writing; the "Fragments" echo Burton, Chesterfield, Burke, Byron, Campbell, Milton, Shakespeare, Sheridan, Coleridge, Scott, the *Arabian Nights*, and classical mythology. *Mardi* disconcerted most of its readers by its curious mythopœic, allegorical, discursive, and whimsical story, and by its lavish, unassimilated, literary sophistication. Melville's reputation drooped, and he needed money; his first son Malcolm had just been born.

As the Duyckincks' *Cyclopædia of American Literature* puts it, apparently ignoring every deeper element in Melville's nature, "Mr Melville, who throughout his literary career has had the good sense never to argue with the public . . . lost no time in recovering his position by a return to the agreeable narrative which had first gained him his laurels."[5] *Redburn* came out late in 1849, *White Jacket* in 1850. Melville disparaged both as pot-boilers but both were, justly, well received: they have a force and directness which are points of support after the fantastics of *Mardi* and before the metaphysics of *Moby Dick* and *Pierre*, and which earned him from the *Literary World* the title of "the De Foe of the Ocean."

In October 1849 he sailed for Europe. His *Journal of a Visit to London and the Continent, 1849–1850* abounds in observations relevant to the novels and stories, as for instance his meeting with the negro who re-appears in *Billy Budd*—"more than forty years ago . . . on the terrace at Greenwich, a Baltimore negro, a Trafalgar man." The Hotel de Cluny in Paris, "the vaults of the old Roman palace of Thermes," and the paintings of Versailles are worked up in *Moby Dick*, and the etiquette of brandy gives him the ninth chapter of *Israel Potter*. The three kings of Cologne and the heights of Ehrenbreitstein recur more than once later. In London, the Lord Mayor's feast prompts "Rich Man's Crumbs," a visit to the Lyceum reappears in "The Two Temples," and the Crusaders' effigies in the Temple Church, the Cigar Divan in the Strand, and a dinner in Elm Court in the Temple combine in "The Paradise of Bachelors." He buys *The Aristocracy of England* (used early in *Pierre*), an eighteenth-century map of London for a proposed "Revolutionary Narrative of the Beggar" (i.e. *Israel Potter*), and Lavater's *Physiognomy* (often cited later). Moreover, his growing antiquarianism of taste is reflected in purchases of Jonson, Beaumont and Fletcher, Browne, and *Hudibras*; he

turns over "noble old works" at the booksellers'. For the
first time he reads Lamb *in extenso*, and *Tristram Shandy*.
In particular, he buys that "wonderful thing . . . most
wondrous book . . . marvellous book," the *Confessions of
an English Opium-Eater*: Fedallah in *Moby Dick* is almost
certainly prompted by the mysterious Malay who called
at De Quincey's cottage and later haunted his dreams.
Melville would find congenial De Quincey's phantas-
magoric but vivid reminiscence, with its ample range of
speculation, its ingenious analogies, its florid style, its
clash of high-flown fancies and prosaic reality, its intimate manner, its meditation on "*the burden of the Incom-
municable*," its record of terrible poverty in a harsh city,
its taste for "German metaphysics," its reflexions on
spontaneous alcoholic combustion so relevant to the
identical phenomenon in *Redburn*, and the opium-dreams
which recall the reveries of ch. cxix, on "Dreams," in
Mardi. The other noteworthy feature of Melville's journal
is his addiction to metaphysics. "Riding on the German
horse again" during his ocean crossing, he "talked metaphysics continually," "talked metaphysics till midnight,"
"talked high German metaphysics," at times "under the
influence of the whisky." The comment, "Discussed 'Fixed
Fate, Free Will, Foreknowledge absolute' &c. with Mr
Adler" (his travelling companion, the German philologist
George Adler), sounds like the germ of ch. xlvi, "The Mat-
Maker," in *Moby Dick*. In short, the journal represents
the powerful crescendo of interests, worldly, transcendental, and aesthetic, which was giving Melville's mind so
dramatic a development around his thirtieth year. The
"Dreams" chapter in *Mardi* indicates the conflux which
produced *Moby Dick*; it culminates like a foretaste of
Whitman:

As the great Mississippi musters his watery nations;
Ohio, with all his leagued streams; Missouri, bringing
down in torrents the clans from the highlands;

Arkansas, his Tartar rivers from the plain;—so, with
all the past and present pouring in me, I roll down my
billow from afar.

In a famous letter to Hawthorne, in June 1851, Melville
referred to his sense of a fateful dynamic:

Until I was twenty-five, I had no development at all.
From my twenty-fifth year I date my life. Three weeks
have scarcely passed, at any time between then and
now, that I have not unfolded within myself. But I
feel that I am now come to the inmost leaf of the bulb,
and that shortly the flower must fall to the mould.[6]

In the summer of 1850 he and his family moved to
Pittsfield in Massachusetts; Hawthorne was seven miles
away at Lenox. A delightful situation arose when a pseu-
donymous review of impassioned admiration for *Mosses
from an Old Manse* reached Hawthorne in August. By a
strange coincidence Hawthorne wrote to Evert Duyckinck
expressing in one and the same letter his "very great
pleasure" in his unknown reviewer and his "progressive
appreciation" of Melville as a writer. When these two
were found to be the same person, Hawthorne and
Melville became friends and Sophia Hawthorne wrote
an interesting account to her mother:

Mr Melville is a person of great ardor & simplicity.
He is all on fire with the subject that interests him. It
rings through his frame like a cathedral bell. His
truth and honesty shine out at every point. At the same
time he sees things artistically, as you perceive in his
books. . . . We find him a man with a true, warm
heart, and a soul and an intellect,—with life to his
finger-tips; earnest, sincere, and reverent; very tender
and *modest*. And I am not sure that he is not a very
great man. . . . He is tall and erect, with an air free,
brave, and manly. When conversing, he is full of
gesture and force, and loses himself in his subject.
There is no grace nor polish. Once in a while, his

animation gives place to a singularly quiet expression,
. . . an indrawn, dim look, but which at the same time
makes you feel that he is at that instant taking deepest
note of what is before him. It is a strange, lazy glance,
but with a power in it quite unique. It does not seem to
penetrate through you, but to take you into himself.[7]

In October 1851, in which month Melville's second
son Stanwix was born, *Moby Dick* appeared. Together
with some strong rejections of it there were strong
praises, particularly in the first American reviews. Business was initially fair; 2,000 copies were sold in five
months. But later reviews were hostile; annual sales
averaged, over the next decade, only 123, and during the
twenty-five years after that only 22. By 1887 fewer than
4,000 had been sold in all, as against the 200,000 of *Ben
Hur* in 1887 and 290,000 in 1888. America needed only
one reprint between 1851 and 1892 (Harper's, 1863),
England only one between 1851 and 1902 (Bentley's,
1853). Melville's masterpiece all but effected his eclipse.
Pierre (1852) made things still worse, and Melville had
a difficult decade, his eyes painful from overstrain, ill-
health impairing his once great vitality, his money low,
and his family growing (by 1855 two daughters were
added to the two sons). His temperament may have
suffered after so much exhaustingly original composition,
but the evidence seems inadequate for the gloomy picture
of domestic bitterness, neurasthenia, despair, and in-
cipient insanity which is still too commonly accepted. He
farmed, with fluctuating success, and until 1857 he
wrote professionally, often very well indeed; *Israel Potter*
(1855) and the best of the *Piazza Tales* (1856) claim their
place with his finest and most characteristic work. The
Journal of a Visit to Europe and the Levant, of 1856-7 (first
published 1935), shows a highly intelligent and formid-
able power, and *The Confidence-Man* (1857), though not
quite successful, is inventive, surprising, and acute.

But Melville's thirty-four remaining years passed in growing obscurity. He lectured without great success for three seasons (1858–60); now and then vainly sought official posts; and during the Civil War wrote the poems published in *Battle-Pieces* (1866). At last, in December 1866, he became an inspector of customs in New York, and he remained so until 1885. In 1867 his son Malcolm was found shot, apparently from a suicidal impulse. In 1876 appeared *Clarel*, a philosophical narrative poem based on his Near-East visit twenty years earlier—"several thousand lines, eminently adapted for unpopularity," he called it to James Billson, an English admirer.[8] In 1888 he arranged a limited private printing of *John Marr and other Sailors* and began *Billy Budd*, which he finished in April 1891. Five months later, on 28 September, he died in New York, having prepared a private publication of *Timoleon*, his last volume of poems.

During these later years his intellectual concerns are more notable than outward events. They consist of the poems (especially *Clarel*, with its discussions of faiths and doubts), the markings he made in books he was reading, and *Billy Budd*. His book-markings are of two main kinds—on independence of spirit, and on metaphysical and religious speculations. The former concentrate on resigned but not tragic acceptance of the world's incomprehension, and on patient spiritual autonomy. The latter show him severe on optimists (Emerson gets some cuts) and earnestly agnostic in the best nineteenth-century way. Surviving for forty years his short spell of fame, he lived in a private way, quietly, but companionably. In 1873 he marked a stanza of John Heywood—

> In such things as we cannot flee,
> But needs they must enduréd be,
> Let wise contentment be decree,
> Make virtue of necessity;
>   Be merry, friends.[9]

In 1885 he wrote of himself as "neither pessimist nor optimist," though preferring pessimism as "a counterpoise to the exorbitant hopefulness, juvenile and shallow, that makes such a bluster in these days."[10] He kept up a friendly though reduced correspondence, dedicated two volumes of poems affectionately to his wife (with whom his earlier relationship was perhaps uneasy with the uneasiness of genius), confined his misanthropic inclinations to underlinings in Balzac or Schopenhauer,[11] and finally, in *Billy Budd*, made a statement on life and death, evil and good, that affects one like the end of *Samson Agonistes*. To be too cheerful, or too cheerless, about Melville's later years would both be equally wrong. The spirit that after the stresses, the almost uncontrollable excitements, and the disappointments of Melville's middle life could write the "Epilogue" to *Clarel* or the account of Billy Budd's death was certainly resilient. In the Catskill eagle, diving into gloom but rising also into sunlight,[12] and in the Galapagos tortoises, dark one side, bright the other,[13] he had imaged the complementary faces of life. This complementary life he seems to have made his own, in fact as well as imagination.

REFERENCES

1. G. S. Fraser, *Ezra Pound*, in "Writers and Critics," 1960, p. 1.
2. Metcalf, p. 92.
3. *M.D.*, ch. xxiv (st. ed., I. 139).
4. Leyda, II. 640.
5. *Cyclopædia of American Literature*, edd. E. A. and G. L. Duyckinck, 1855, II. 673.
6. *Letters*, p. 130.
7. Metcalf, pp. 91–3.
8. *Letters*, p. 275.
9. Leyda, II. 736.
10. *Letters*, p. 277.
11. Leyda, II. 830, 832.
12. *M.D.*, ch. xcv (st. ed., ch. xcvi).
13. "The Encantadas," Sketch Second.

B

CHAPTER II

TYPEE AND *OMOO*

The first two novels spring from an energy working freshly, humorously, intelligently, and unencumbered by complexities. They show an unusual poetic charm at one end of the spectrum, force and the drama of violent action at the other; and Melville handles the rhythm and pace of his prose admirably. What they share is evident enough—exotic material, youthful vitality, independence of mind, a natural capacity to write. They differ, however, more than the practice of coupling them together would suggest—in the nature of their experience and feelings, the strength of their criticism, and the stages they mark in Melville's evolution. *Omoo* is much nearer to *Mardi* than *Typee* is, though no reader of *Omoo* could actually have predicted *Mardi*. Most readers will hold *Typee* the more affectionately in mind; yet *Omoo* in its more miscellaneous course has striking signs of power.

Uncomplicated yarns though they are (and one is glad to have them so), *Typee* and *Omoo* remain meaningfully in the mind, not because Melville has worked as hard as later he was to do—they flow easily—but because, like the later life of shipboard or the Mississippi, their worlds are singularly well evoked. Sophia Hawthorne touched agreeably on the particular charm of *Typee*:

I have just read again *Typee*. It is a *true history*, yet how poetically told—the divine beauty of the scene, the lovely faces & forms,—the peace & good will—& all this golden splendor & enchantment glowing before the dark refrain constantly brought as a background—

the fear of being killed & eaten—the cannibalism in the olive tinted Apollos around him—the unfathomable mystery of their treatment of him.[1]

This double emotion is peculiarly haunting, on the one hand paradisal, on the other nervous and forlorn. One would not minimise the interest of the early chapters on and off ship; from the first sentences the pages tingle and the writing throughout the escape and flight is vivacious. Yet the central significance is in the valley of the Typees, given an intense separateness by the nightmarish dangers involved in arriving in and departing from it. The harsh irreversible journey, followed by the conclusive descent of the precipitous waterfall, is the initiatory means of putting Typee life into its serene isolation, just as finally Tommo's growing hysteria of loneliness and his desperate break through the obstructing natives are, as it were, a violence of being reintroduced into the "real" world. These two definitive events frame that state of nature which so idyllically contrasts with "civilisation" yet whose unintellectuality and dreamlike inconsequentiality are a life to which, as D. H. Lawrence was to insist, the Westerner cannot really commit himself.

In describing and in giving information Melville is strikingly good. Much though he derives from authorities on Polynesia, he brings to his accounts a spiritedness which makes *Typee*, to quote Clark Russell, the English dedicatee of *John Marr*, "an accurate study rendered romantic by the warm imagination through which it passes." The account of "tappa"-making is a model of lucidity and animation;[2] the episode of Kory-Kory's fire-lighting shows Melville's command of effect.

At first Kory-Kory goes to work quite leisurely, but gradually quickens his pace, and waxing warm in the employment, drives the stick furiously along the smoking channel, plying his hands to and fro with amazing rapidity, the perspiration starting from every pore. As he approaches the climax of his effort, he pants and gasps for breath, and his eyes almost start from their sockets with the violence of his exertions. This is the critical stage of the operation: all his previous labours are vain if he cannot sustain the rapidity of the movement until the reluctant spark is produced. Suddenly he stops, becomes perfectly motionless. His hands still retain their hold of the smaller stick, which is pressed convulsively against the further end of the channel among the fine powder there accumulated, as if he had just pierced through and through some little viper that was wriggling and struggling to escape from his clutches. The next moment a delicate wreath of smoke curls spirally into the air, the heap of dusty particles glows with fire, and Kory-Kory, almost breathless, dismounts.[3]

The prose is slightly stylised, but attractively so and without detriment. Melville's power at his best, of having the reader there beside him, is hallucinatory.

In *The Young Rebel in American Literature*, Carl Bode observes that the American writers best known to the world represent a tradition of anti-materialism and nonconformity. In this tradition Melville from the start participates. The deserters from the *Dolly* arrive in the valley in a state of ignorance made worse by terrifying hearsay (a situation typified when Tommo awakes from an "appalling dream" prompted by his fears, and finds flower-decked girls surrounding him):[4] they in fact exchange the "advanced" primitivism of whale-fishing under a brutal captain "beyond law and equity" for the Stone-Age primitivism of happy anarchism under a noble-savage chief who does the minimum of ruling. Against the exacerbated complexity of social organisation at home are set the unfettered naturalness of sexuality, the light authority and untroubled obedience of political order; against competitive exertion are set easy satisfaction and sociability; against aggressiveness, the ludicrously trivial war-making of Typees and Happars.

Yet it is less in confrontations of that kind than in its poetic and imaginative beauty that the book survives. Other travellers, Dana very powerfully among them, had made Melville's points about the natural happiness of Marquesan life, and against the impact of trade and missions, yet they are not, not even Dana, so widely read. From the first encounter with the Typee children the book has a tenderness for this harmless existence, which rises into a captivating and appealing sensuality when the native girls are described, from the swimming "whinhenies" who board the *Dolly* to the bathing parties and that appealing romantic evocation Fayaway—phantom, one would write, had not Melville firmly declared her "no fancy sketch." This side of the book has a sweetness of sentiment doubtless no greater than the originals justified, and little harmed by the slight coyness which nineteenth-century literary behaviour inevitably assumed with such a subject. The creditable thing is that Melville brings over his impressions so well. It is true that not all his effects, however vividly rendered, are from his own observations: some of the most brilliant, here and elsewhere, derive from his reading (the threatened flogging and the yard-arm fall in *White Jacket*, for instance; the try-works and whale-nursery in *Moby Dick*; the whole of "Benito Cereno"; and so on). But this does not matter; as Dryden remarks of Jonson, "he invades his authors like a monarch; and what would be theft in other poets, is only victory in him." The creative assimilation is alive, and if, for example, Mehevi's accoutrements owe much to "sources", he is still amply present:

His aspect was imposing. The splendid long drooping tail-feathers of the tropical bird, thickly interspersed with the gaudy plumage of the cock, were disposed in an immense upright semi-circle upon his head, their lower extremities being fixed in a crescent of guinea-beads which spanned his forehead. Around his neck were several enormous necklaces of boars' tusks, polished like ivory, and disposed in such a manner as that the longest and largest were upon his capacious chest. Thrust forward through the large apertures in his ears were two small and finely shaped sperm-whale teeth, presenting their cavities in front, stuffed with freshly plucked leaves, and curiously wrought at the other end into strange little images and devices.[5]

Omoo looks, on the face of it, much the same thing. It has the same Polynesian landscapes in the lush nineteenth-century style. It has, though more fully and passionately stated, the theme of corruption following on "civilisation." It equally weaves first- and second-hand material into a unified fabric; affairs on the *Julia* and *La Reine Blanche*, or in the British Consulate and the Calabooza Beretanee, are autobiographically authentic; Jim the port pilot, Wilson the acting consul, the visiting French priests, Long Ghost, Zeke and Shorty, can all be vouched for as direct experience, as can the state of Tahiti, whereas the excellent chapter on the coco-palm is from Ellis's *Polynesian Researches*. But to sift the ingredients is unprofitable. What is more useful is to observe the differentiations from *Typee*. First, *Omoo* more strongly conveys the web of life, substituting for Happy-Valley isolation a narrative of picaresque hazards and companionships. Secondly, it more evidently prefigures Melville's later work, and is, in a way, premonitory. And thirdly, it brings one harder up against reality. *Typee* is like a living spell—"a magic mirror," with Melville "watching this strange delicious world with intent, water-blue eyes," as Lewis Mumford calls it.[6] That is not the effect of *Omoo*. What is notable is the spare, telling style Melville can manage:

It was in the middle of a bright tropical afternoon that we made good our escape from the bay. The vessel we sought lay with her main-topsail aback about a league from the land, and was the only object that broke the broad expanse of the ocean. On approaching, she turned out to be a small, slatternly-looking craft, her hull and spars a dingy black, rigging all slack and bleached nearly white, and everything denoting an ill state of affairs aboard. The four boats hanging over the bulwarks proclaimed her a whaler. Leaning carelessly over the bulwarks were the sailors, wild, haggard-looking fellows in Scotch caps and faded blue frocks; some of them with cheeks of a mottled bronze, to which sickness soon changes the rich berry-brown of a sea-man's complexion in the tropics.[7]

That simple but masterly assurance, though with a subtler imagination, was to appear later in "Benito Cereno."

The first twenty-seven chapters are among the best in nautical literature, with the vigorous and interesting realism to be resumed in *Redburn*. "A Scene in the Fore-castle"[8] is sharply and powerfully defined, and Melville's skill in communication can be observed in the latter half of the sixth chapter, when the captain's shore expedition, in all the proper diminution of its senseless activity, is surveyed in the clear precision of Long Ghost's telescope. Elsewhere also the style works with marked efficacy:

One afternoon there was a mighty queer noise aloft, which set the men running in every direction. It was the main-top-gallant mast. Crash! it broke off just over the cap, and held there by the rigging dashed with every roll from side to side, with all the hamper that belonged to it. The yard hung by a hair, and at every pitch thumped against the cross-trees; while the sail streamed in ribbons, and the loose ropes coiled, and thrashed the air like whip-lashes. "Stand from under!" and down came the rattling blocks, like so many shot. The yard, with a snap and a plunge, went hissing into the sea, disappeared, and shot its full length out again. The crest of a great wave then broke over it —the ship rushed by—and we saw the stick no more.[9]

One can see in *Omoo* the potential of later novels. The account of Bembo and his harpooning[10] has a strength which might belong to *Moby Dick*; *Redburn* and *White Jacket* are clearly not far away from these early chapters; and, more surprisingly, *Mardi* is uncertainly foreshadowed in the strange musical names, the unfettered wanderings, the island hospitalities on which is strung an anthology of social manners, and the sense of Tahiti as a testing-ground for the confusions and interspersions of peoples, morals, and faiths. One sentence even gives a foretaste of *Mardi*'s style—"Fair dawned, over the hills of Martair, the jocund morning of our hunt."[11] If Smollett can preside, so too, it seems, can Ossian, and the difference between this and the realism quoted above is not reassuring. The conjunction of influences is a pointer to Melville's susceptibility to others' styles, and influences in a weltering abundance were to be the mark of his next book. But *Omoo* remains picaresque, entertaining, and real, if flagging now and then into the haphazard; it has, as Lewis Mumford comments, "the sharpness, the force, the exaggeration of character which the eighteenth century had in its satiric artists; and every episode is carried off with a dry discretion."[12]

REFERENCES

1. Metcalf, p. 91.
2. *T.*, ch. xix.
3. *T.*, ch. xiv.
4. *T.*, ch. xi.
5. *Ibid.*
6. Lewis Mumford, *Herman Melville*, 1929, pp. 72–3.
7. *O.*, ch. i.
8. *O.*, ch. iv.
9. *O.*, ch. xvi.
10. *O.*, ch. xix.
11. *O.*, ch. lvii, first sentence.
12. Lewis Mumford, *Herman Melville*, p. 84.

CHAPTER III

MARDI: AND A VOYAGE THITHER

Mardi, in effect three books in one, if not three and a half, is hard to operate upon critically. In *The Two Exiles—D. H. Lawrence and Byron*, Graham Hough has observed of Byron that at least superficially he is "a mass of romantic fantasy, historic and geographical self-dramatisation, irony with sentiment—and apparently no guiding principle whatever . . . no machinery at all for exploring an unknown situation. He has not only little self-knowledge; he has no technique at all for acquiring any." This may certainly be said of Melville in *Mardi*. But it would need a proviso—that the very conduct of this curious novel (and later of *Pierre* too), manifold in manner and material, uncertain and uncontrollable in aim, seems at this point in his evolution actually to be Melville's form of guiding principle, his machinery for exploring the unknown and acquiring self-knowledge. He recognised that this had been its use to him, for he wrote to Evert Duyckinck, "Had I not written & published 'Mardi,' in all likelihood, I would not be as wise as I am now, or may be."[1] The novel is not the finished result but the impulse and process. The reasons lie in Melville's strongly experimental temperament, which makes each novel different from the others (and several drastically different), and in his puzzlement as to how novels should relate to life. Repeatedly, in *Pierre*, *The Confidence-Man*, and *Billy Budd*, for instance, he stresses that art falsifies experience by imposing shape and logic.

With this, the rapid unfolding within himself which he described to Hawthorne had much to do. He told John

Murray that the main inducement to the strange course
Mardi was assuming was "the reiterated imputation of
being a romancer in disguise," which had "pricked" him
into a resolution to show that "a *real* romance of mine is
no Typee or Omoo, & is made of different stuff altogether."[2] But secondly, he explains, he was driven by an
uncontrollable impulse:

> Proceeding in my narrative of *facts*, I began to feel an
> incurible [sic] distaste for the same; & a longing to
> plume my pinions for a flight, & felt irked, cramped &
> fettered by plodding along with dull commonplaces.[3]

It is this new element which was to play havoc, if fas-
cinating havoc, with *Mardi* and *Pierre*, and to give *Moby
Dick* its complex suprarational power, its extravagance
for better or worse, and, in short, its greatness. The most
interesting comments on the result are Melville's own,
first in *Mardi*, when the philosopher Babbalanja describes
the dead writer Lombardo and his "grand" work
"Koztanza";[4] secondly in a letter to *Mardi*'s London
publisher Bentley; and thirdly in *Pierre*, discussing the
relationship between fiction and life.

First, for Lombardo: he, Babbalanja explains, wrote
from need of money, but also from "a full heart:—brim-
ful, bubbling, sparkling; and running over."[5] Urged by
an unconscious force, a "sleep-walking of the mind,"[6]
"he was not his own master; a mere amanuensis writing
by dictation":

> When Lombardo set about his work, he knew not what
> it would become. He did not build himself in with
> plans; he wrote right on; and so doing, got deeper and
> deeper into himself.[7]

Ignoring the unities, his book derived its form from "one
autocrat within—his crowned and sceptered instinct"[8]
("instincts are prophetic," Melville told Murray in the
letter quoted, "and better than acquired wisdom").
The "Koztanza" expresses the world's diversity:

nothing but episodes; valleys and hills; rivers digress-
ing from plains; vines, roving all over; boulders and
diamonds; flowers and thistles; forests and thickets;
and, here and there, fens and moors. And so, the world
in the Koztanza.[9]

And moreover, the "Koztanza" is symbolic—"things
infinite in the finite; and dualities in unities."[10]

Secondly, the letter to Bentley admits that *Mardi* may
have been "unwise, indiscreet," but continues:

Some of us, My Dear Sir, always have a certain something unmanageable in us, that bids us do this or that,
and be done it must—hit or miss.[11]

This is the "incomprehensible stranger" that Babbalanja
recognises within himself, that makes him "a blind man
pushed from behind . . . yet all the time, this being is I,
myself."[12]

And thirdly, *Pierre* was to comment that the "eternally
unsystematizable elements" of the world do not submit
to the simplifications of the normal novel—"the profounder emanations of the human mind . . . never unravel
their own intricacies, and have no proper endings."[13]
These *donnés* on the novel—its unplanned plenitude,
symbolic significances, unmanageable impulses, and recognition of the "unsystematizable"—are of great importance in the study of Melville.

The early chapters give no open indication of anything
other than nautical material, though Melville's mind
certainly spills more unpredictably forth, having enriched
itself in contact with New York literary circles. But in
March 1848 Evert Duyckinck wrote to George that the
new work "in the poetry and wildness of the thing will be
ahead of Typee & Omoo." The adventure-story intended in mid-1847 developed into a romance fantasy,
with the quest for the white maiden Yillah under the
spell of the dark enchantress Hautia. With the pressure of
Rabelais's influence and the events of 1848, in America

and Europe, it exploded further into a satiric voyage-
quest like that of Panurge, Pantagruel, and Father John
after the oracle of Bacbuc. Ingredients less likely to
cohere one could hardly find, but coherence was not
Melville's concern. The result, to quote Hawthorne, is

> a rich book, with depths here and there that compel a
> man to swim for his life. . . . It is so good that one
> scarcely pardons the writer for not having brooded
> long over it, so as to make it a great deal better.[14]

The early nautical part needs less comment than what
follows; the observations one may select from many possible ones concern the sophisticated literary manner, and
the interspersed metaphysical speculations. Erudition is
richly sprinkled in, with imitations of Burton and Browne
(and later of many others); ch. xiii invokes Browne's
Vulgar Errors and audibly parodies his style. The narrator's companion, old Jarl the Skyeman, owes something
to antique sea-heroics; "Ah! how the old Sagas run
through me!" the narrator exclaims in describing him.[15]
Melville was in fact reading Esaias Tegner's *Frithiof's
Saga*, that sentimentalised rendering of *Frithiof the Bold*
from which come Jarl's Vikingism, some verbal details,
and doubtless his name. Already this is not merely *Omoo*
continued. Similar sources to *Omoo*'s admittedly are
used, in particular F. D. Bennett's *Whaling Voyage round
the Globe*, *1833–1836*, from which derive the chapters on
the shovel-nosed shark,[16] the sword-fish with its attacks on
ships and its name "Xiphius Platypterus,"[17] and the
striking account of phosphorescence.[18] Bennett probably
also gave the name Hautia, the hibiscus of the Society
Islands. But the effect is different from *Omoo*: Melville
is less relating an adventure than creating the world of
the sea, with an abundance which turns naturalism into
a kind of magic, an enchantment of the strangeness and
plenitude of nature. This points towards *Moby Dick*, as do
also the speculative interests. The comments on seraphs

and sharks as aspects of one Creator,[19] and elsewhere on the interrelated orders of the sea,[20] show a more ranging enquiry than heretofore. The "things infinite in the finite" hint their presence.

From ch. xli the romance takes its "unmanageable" course. Having rescued from sacrifice the mysterious Yillah, and killed her guardian the high-priest Aleema, the narrator lands as the demigod Taji in the fanciful Polynesian archipelago of Mardi. Yillah soon vanishes, spirited away by Hautia, and Taji seeks her throughout the islands, pursued alike by Aleema's three avenging sons and by Hautia's three messengers, who haunt him with symbolic flower-messages. Hautia's bower-of-bliss allurements fail, and Taji, glimpsing the drowned Yillah floating away on a subterranean current, takes to the water in heroic distraction and, still pursued by the avengers, sails on "over an endless sea." What this all means matters little, since one is not sufficiently affected by it to mind much one way or the other, and the critics are at variance. But, not to shirk the problem entirely, it may be surmised that in a Blakian way Taji rescues joy from the religion which would sacrifice her, by rejecting religion and being thereafter hounded by religion's agents. The joy he cherishes is distinct from the sensuality which tempts him, sensuality which may momentarily be mistaken for joy (Hautia and Yillah being strangely connected) but which in reality destroys joy utterly. This may be Melville's meaning. Or it may not.

At any rate, it is evident how deeply and indeed questionably he has succumbed to "the romance & poetry of the thing"; this is the realm of dream-fantasy so insidiously potent with the Romantics. Ossian is not far away; Melville bought *Fingal* in 1848 and noted "An admirable *nature* is observable all over Ossian: The pathos —none can speak it." Whether he had yet read Keats or Shelley is uncertain, but *Endymion*'s enchanted quest comes to mind, and so do *Alastor*'s Indian maiden

vanishing from the Vale of Cashmire, and the hero in
pursuit reaching the melancholy shore, with his

> restless impulse to embark,
> And meet lone Death on the drear ocean's waste.

Hautia's allurements may owe something to Southey's
Thalaba, as the *New Monthly Magazine* of April 1849
suggested. In a "voluptuous vale" of flowers and music
Thalaba is offered wine and "odorous fruits," and tempted
by seductive dancing, but he is saved from surrender by
thinking of his lost Oneiza, who then appears fleeing
from the sensualists. Thalaba and Taji seem linked by
the story in *Mardi*, offered as a parallel to Taji's, in
which, "camel-like laden with woe," the youth Ozanna
finds (but in this case too late) his lost love transformed
into one of Hautia's thralls.[21] "Oneiza" and "Ozanna"
are oddly similar, the absurd "camel-like" suggests
Southey's orientalism, and Melville's lavishness resembles
Southey's, though greatly outdoing it. *Mardi*'s flower-
apparatus too may reflect Southey, but it owes its symbolism to Frances Osgood's *Poetry of Flowers and Flowers of
Poetry* (1841).[22] Hautia herself is generically akin to
Spenser's Acrasia or false Florimel, Coleridge's Geral-
dine, Keats's Lamia ("snake and victim; life ebbing out
from me, to her"),[23] or, in Wieland's *Oberon*, Queen
Almansaris, who intercepts Huon's flower-messages, en-
tices him with dancers and wine, and tempts him with
marriage, a throne, and glory (as Hautia offers "Beauty,
Health, Wealth, Long Life, and the Last Lost Hope of
Man.")[24] As for Yillah, she belongs with a host of Romantic visionary maidens. Melville's brother-in-law, Lemuel
Shaw jr., borrowed La Motte Fouqué's *Undine* from the
Boston Athenæum in 1847, perhaps on his behalf. One
of the famous Romantic fantasies, this tells of Hulde-
brand, a wandering knight, and Undine, the water-
sprite who must marry a mortal to gain a soul: Arnold's
"Forsaken Merman" is the same *genre* of story. Hulde-

brand leaves Undine for his former betrothed, but on his wedding-night she visits him as a ghost and he dies embracing her. Yillah's name and significance suggests Mrs Osgood's "lily" ("Purity and Modesty"); she reflects an Undine-like mystery or, for example (instances could be multiplied), the maiden

> half-veiled from view . . .
> In the clear crystal of a brook

for whom in Thomas Moore's *Loves of the Angels* the first angel leaves Heaven. She is elusively evoked:

> Of her beauty I say nothing. It was that of a crystal lake in a fathomless wood: all light and shade; full of fleeting revealings; now shadowed in depths; now sunny in dimples; but all sparkling and shifting, and blending together. But her wild beauty was a veil to things still more strange. As often she gazed so earnestly into my eyes, like some pure spirit looking far down into my soul, and seeing therein some upturned faces, I started in amaze, and asked what spell was on me.[25]

The voyagings, quests through exotic islands or subterranean waters, aspirations for a visionary maiden, hauntings, fleeings from mankind like those of Byron's

> wanderers o'er Eternity
> Whose bark drives on and on, and anchor'd ne'er
> shall be

—these are elements of a Romantic mythopœia to which Melville does not valuably add, since his allegory is too elusive, his fairy-tale too absurd. But he achieves beauty at times, as when Taji approaches Hautia's island:

> Lo you! the glittering foam all round its white marge; where, forcing themselves underneath the coral ledge, and up through its crevices, in fountains, the blue billows gush. . . . Round about the isle, like winged rainbows, shoals of dolphins were leaping over floating

fragments of wrecks:—dark-green, long-haired ribs
and keels of canoes. . . . Over and over they sprang:
from east to west: rising and setting: many suns in a
moment; while all the sea, like a harvest plain, was
stacked with their glittering sheaves of spray. And far
down, fathoms on fathoms, flitted rainbow-hues:—
as seines-full of mermaids; half-screening the bones of
the drowned. . . . We now took our way by a winding
vale; where, by sweet-scented hedges, flowed the blue-
braided brooks; their tributaries, rivulets of violets,
meandering through the meads. . . . Here, the peach
tree showed her thousand cheeks of down, kissed often
by the wooing winds; there, in swarms, the yellow
apples hived, like golden bees upon the boughs; here,
from the kneeling, fainting trees, thick fell the cherries,
in great drops of blood; and here the pomegranate,
with cold rind and sere, deep pierced by bills of birds,
revealed the mellow of its ruddy core.[26]

Lavish rather than sensitive, that may perhaps be faulted,
since it fails in any deeply imaginative correspondence
between word and meaning. But done less lavishly it
would less reveal its astounding commitment to its fantasy. The Yillah-Hautia story, indulgent, abundant, and
ornate, is in the *genre* of *The Faerie Queene*; both have a
dreaming wandering course, a refined richness, a theme of
innocence, enchantment, and quest, an allegory naïve
and elusive, a symbolism observed or neglected at will.

This search is involved in another, that of King Media,
the philosopher Babbalanja, the chronicler Mohi, and
the poet Yoomy, for wisdom. The whimsical chapter-
headings suggest the prototype quest for the Holy Bottle
in Rabelais's fourth and fifth books. The episodes lead to
the land of Serenia, the Christian ideal in practice, and
under the thinnest of satirical disguises they include
observations on Europe and America, the 1848 revolu-
tions, the Chartist movement, the Mexican War (1846–

1848), the Oregon boundary question, the Californian gold-rush (1848), and the 1848 Presidential campaign which brought the slavery problem forward. "This new world, here sought," Melville claims of these interrelated themes, "is the world of mind."[27] He was currently reading Shakespeare, Montaigne, Burton, Hartley, Coleridge, and Seneca, whose *Morals* translated by L'Estrange is the "marvellous book" Babbalanja praises as containing Christian ethics independently of Christian revelation.[28] He was following scientific discussions and includes in *Mardi* extravaganzas on geology and on physiology.[29] The name Taji probably comes from an astronomical discussion between Edward Everett and Le Verrier on "les comètes de Taïje et de Vico," and the names of Mardi and Media from Charles Anthon's *Classical Dictionary* (1845), in which they are a people and a country of Asia. The absurd philosophical terms[30] are from Taylor's translation of Proclus (1816). From Rabelais derive not only the whole scheme but incidents like Oh-Oh's museum,[31] the Minda sorcerers,[32] and the interview with Hivohitee.[33] Melville had done nothing earlier comparable to this wide-garnering harvest. If the result in *Mardi* is unmanageably miscellaneous, "the world of mind" was henceforth to be his concern— magnificently allied with nature in *Moby Dick*, virtually monopolising *Pierre*.

The philosophical search tests codes of life, and leads to the ideals of Alma (Christ) in Serenia, for all except Taji. Taji ceases to count almost as soon as he lands, but through the others Melville has a device for multiple judgment, Media being the central point of common sense, Mohi the traditionalist, Babbalanja the searching sceptic, Yoomy the dreamy romantic. Unfortunately, so confusing are the positions inspected, so whimsical the by-play, so sophomoric the epigrams and humorous sallies, that the effects of the synoptic device are largely dissipated. Lewis Mumford has put this most charitably,

C

observing that "Melville is so happy that he does not notice one cannot always share the emotion with him."[34] The enthusiasm one can take pleasure in, while nevertheless feeling that so much effervescence of notion is more to the author's satisfaction than the reader's.

The most notable positions are one, political-moral, the other, ethical-religious. The former is Babbalanja's discourse on slavery,[35] a grave and ultimately passionate appeal for humanity. The latter is Babbalanja's search for an ethic combining head and heart. This search was Melville's own life-long interest, and it may have been the Unitarian strain so distinguished in New England life, and represented by his wife and father-in-law, that prompted him to admire first Seneca's noble stoicism[36] and then the undogmatic ethical Christianity of Serenia.[37] This is in the great tradition of the nineteenth-century enquiring mind, and its expression moves as literature and doctrine together. This position, and the contrasted one in which Taji, "the unreturning wanderer, . . . my own soul's emperor," commits "the last, last crime" by leaving Serenia for the Byronic enterprise of desperation, are relevant later in the assessment of *Moby Dick*. One side of Melville undoubtedly wants to make this Byronic gesture: the end of *Mardi*, though extravagantly melodramatic, has a remarkable force and pulse, a mad but genuine poetry dispelling the impatience which, on the face of it, one has every right to feel. Yet criticism loses balance if "Romantic Agony" is read as the whole theme. *Moby Dick* is the story of Ahab but the story also of Ishmael the redeemed survivor, of Queequeg the noble savage, of nature's grandeur and fertility, of the heart's affections as well as revenge. And Taji, whose reduction from convincing whaleman to possessed phantom typifies the book's weaker fantasies, does not embody Melville's major intuition. In *Mardi*, as against defiance and despair, there are comedy, faith, and affection; as Taji flees, the young Yoomy is seen buoying the old Mohi up through the waves. Media and his companions contradict Taji's fatalism. This seems to be Melville's intention, despite the welter of material which defeats one's best attempts to see *Mardi* steadily and see it whole.

REFERENCES

1. *Letters*, p. 96.
2. *Letters*, p. 70.
3. *Letters*, p. 70.
4. *M.*, ch. clxxx (st. ed., II. 321).
5. *M.*, *loc. cit.* (st. ed., II. 322).
6. *M.*, *loc. cit.* (st. ed., II. 327).
7. *M.*, *loc. cit.* (st. ed., II. 326).
8. *M.*, *loc. cit.* (st. ed., II. 328).
9. *M.*, *loc. cit.* (st. ed., II. 329).
10. *M.*, *loc. cit.* (st. ed., II. 328).
11. *Letters*, p. 86.
12. *M.*, ch. cxliii (st. ed., II. 156).
13. *P.*, Bk. VII, sect. viii.
14. Metcalf, p. 90.
15. *M.*, ch. iii (st. ed., I. 13).
16. *M.*, ch. xviii (st. ed., I. 61).
17. *M.*, ch. xxxii (st. ed., I. 118).
18. *M.*, ch. xxxviii, "The Sea on Fire" (st. ed., I. 140).
19. *M.*, ch. xiii (st. ed., I. 47).
20. *M.*, e.g. chs. xviii, xxxii, xxxviii, xxxix, xlviii (st. ed., I. 61, 118, 140, 144, 172).
21. *M.*, ch. cxciii (st. ed., II. 392).
22. Merrell R. Davis, "Flower Symbolism in *Mardi*," in *Modern Language Quarterly*, 1941, II. 625–38.
23. *M.*, ch. cxcv (st. ed., II. 397).
24. *M.*, ch. cxciv (st. ed., II. 396).
25. *M.*, ch. xlix (st. ed., I. 177).
26. *M.*, ch. cxcii (st. ed., II. 387–388).
27. *M.*, ch. clxix (st. ed., II. 276).
28. *M.*, ch. cxxiv (st. ed., II. 79).
29. *M.*, chs. cxxxii, clv (st. ed., II. 111, 214).
30. *M.*, chs. cx, clxxi (st. ed., II. 22, 284–5).
31. *M.*, chs. cxxii–iii (st. ed., II. 67–76); cp. Rabelais's Library of St Victor, *Gargantua and Pantagruel*, II. vii.
32. *M.*, ch. cxliv (st. ed., II. 162); cp. Rabelais's "furred Law-Cats," *Gargantua and Pantagruel*, v. xii.
33. *M.*, ch. cxvi (st. ed., II. 43); cp. Rabelais's Holy Bottle, *Gargantua and Pantagruel*, v. xlv.
34. Lewis Mumford, *Herman Melville*, p. 92.
35. *M.*, ch. clxii (st. ed., II. 251–252).
36. *M.*, ch. cxxiv (st. ed., II. 77–80).
37. *M.*, ch. clxxxvii (st. ed., II. 364–72).

CHAPTER IV

REDBURN AND WHITE JACKET

Mardi disconcerted the critics. The *Literary Gazette* admitted that "the images are brilliant," but wondered "how aught luminous can be so dark." The London *Athenæum* found it humourless as fun, incomprehensible as allegory, tedious as romance, obscure as prose-poem. Even Melville's own publisher's magazine, *Bentley's Miscellany*, though prepared for "intellectual gambolling," yet confessed to "some dislike to meeting with ideas in so thick a haze that we are unable to perceive distinctly which is which." Melville defended *Mardi* to Bentley, but promised him something easier to follow—

> a thing of a widely different cast from *Mardi*:—a plain, straightforward, amusing narrative of personal experience—the son of a gentleman on his first voyage to sea as a sailor—no metaphysics, no conic-sections, nothing but cakes and ale ["Away with your logic and conic sections!" says Media to Babbalanja in *Mardi*][1] ... what I write I have almost wholly picked up by my own observations under comical circumstances.[2]

"Amusing narrative ... under comical circumstances" suggests the demure irony with which Conrad dedicated *The Secret Agent* to Wells as "this simple tale," for the finest things in *Redburn* are tragic. But perhaps Melville thought, early on, that comedy would predominate.

He disliked *Redburn* and *White Jacket*—"no reputation that can be gratifying to me, can possibly be achieved by either of these books. They are two *jobs*, which I have done for money", he told Lemuel Shaw,[3] though he rejoiced to hear from Dana that the "strange, congenial feelings" with which he had read *Two Years before the Mast* were reciprocated in respect of his own books.[4] Both works are in fact strikingly good. By drastic revulsion, however unwilling, from the manner of *Mardi*, the writing becomes direct, sensitive, and intense, effective as Defoe or Smollett or Dickens are effective. Citing names is not to argue derivation: Melville's stories are recorded originally, with great power, and with strong assimilation of what he has read, heard, and experienced.

The effect of *Redburn* owes much to practical intention, as the letter to Bentley shows, but something perhaps, Leon Howard has suggested, to Melville's imagination sympathetically projected into his young brother Tom, who had gone to sea at sixteen in 1846 and to whom *Redburn* is dedicated. Biographers have often taken *Redburn* as more autobiographical than it is. As with *Pierre*, autobiography is present, but much adjusted. The adjustment in the early chapters is precisely this of the hero's age, since the boyish innocence depicted is hardly that of Melville himself, who was twenty when he first embarked. By projecting the experience back he expresses a sensitiveness unparalleled in his earlier books and rivals the childhood of Moll Flanders, or Colonel Jacque, or David Copperfield, in which unprotected inexperience finds out about life. The early pages admirably evoke the speculations of boyhood out of the details a boy would observe. At times the youthful inexperience may seem overdone, but a tall-story element is always part of Melville's nineteenth-century-American manner, and his comedy often runs to farce, not least in *Moby Dick* and even *Pierre*. Redburn has to play the role of gull, as well as of central consciousness. Indeed, as in Defoe and Dickens, the central consciousness has to learn through the gullibility that makes him vulnerable. Yet, if improbable as facts, the absurdities of his simplicity are entertaining as yarns, and their improbability does not destroy their representative character in the confrontation of well-bred illusion and brutal truth. They are the *sort* of things a sheltered child will undergo. In the scene where Redburn muses on the links with home which Captain Riga represents for him, the warmth of childhood sentiment, though presented for ironic comedy, is caught with moving truth.

If anything is surprising in Redburn's evolution it is not his simplicity but his resilience. This doubtless reflects Melville's relative toughness at twenty. Indeed, Redburn rapidly matures; the childhood eye would not suffice for the personal evil represented in Jackson or the collective evil represented in Liverpool. Yet childhood can be proud and lost and bitter, and these feelings are memorably caught. Redburn in desperate independence flinging his last penny into the river (while admitting he certainly would not have flung his last dollar) and then in his hunger furiously regretting his folly—this has a truth to nature akin to Defoe's.

Few books so well bring home the sense of new experience, of things for the first time unfolded for good or ill, though in its different way *Typee* is a precedent. In *Typee*, misconceptions of savage life are contrasted with what it is—benign and Rousseauistic. In *Redburn* the contrast is reversed. Expectations are deceptive. The "strange, romantic charm" of shipping advertisements and his father's stories becomes briefly real on the sunlit sea— "how grand and majestic, how solitary, and boundless, and beautiful and blue."[5] But by the end of the chapter, "commanded like a slave, and set to work like an ass," Redburn is cleaning chicken-coops. In his imagination Liverpool is romantic; in fact it looks like New York, and it reveals a nightmare of degradation. One recalls Conrad, in *The Nigger of the Narcissus*, on sailors' knowledge of the land—

the frontier of infamy and filth, . . . that border of dirt and hunger, of misery and dissipation, that comes down on all sides to the water's edge of the incorruptible ocean, and is the only thing they know of life, the only thing they see of surrounding land—those life-long prisoners of the sea.

The rendering is cogent, substantial with detail, graphic with particularity. Though Melville is less brilliant, one thinks repeatedly of Dickens. The observation of the pawnbrokers' shops[6] is highly effective, and the undodgeable reality of shipboard life equals, if not surpasses, Smollett and Dana in creating a complete world. In this life there is abundant flavour and character—in Mr Thompson, the Bible-reading cook, packed into his galley and sweating as he reads; Lavender, the steward, with "claret-coloured suits, and snuff-coloured suits, and red velvet vests, and buff-and-brimstone pantaloons, and several full suits of black which, with his dark-coloured face, made him look quite clerical"; Jack Blunt, of the hair-oils and dream book; Larry, the whaleman; Gundeck, the man-o'-war's man; Handsome Mary and her Liverpool boarding house;[7] and the Liverpool scenes and characters altogether.[8] These and others have not only their own features and behaviour but their own worlds and natures. They are created as well as observed. In this regard the most striking achievement is that of Jackson. Dominating, evil, and wasting, he is expressed with a mysterious passion, yet on the whole not, as with Ahab later, with rhetoric and portentousness. Jackson's force, like the book's force, is conveyed concretely, and by Melville's imaginative grandeur the misery of this possessed man is as integral as his moral foulness:

He seldom spoke but to contradict, deride or curse; and all the time, though his face grew thinner and thinner, his eyes seemed to kindle more and more, as if he were going to die out at last, and leave them burning like tapers before a corpse. Though he had never attended churches, and knew nothing about Chris-

tianity, no more than a Malay pirate; and though he
could not read a word, yet he was spontaneously an
atheist and an infidel; and during the long night
watches would enter into arguments to prove that there
was nothing to be believed; nothing to be loved, and
nothing worth living for; but every thing to be hated,
in the wide world. . . . But there seemed even more woe
than wickedness about the man; and his wickedness
seemed to spring from his woe; and for all his hideousness, there was that in his eye at times, that was
ineffably pitiable and touching; and though there were
moments when I almost hated this Jackson, yet I have
pitied no man as I have pitied him.[9]

If Jackson presents personal evil, the dying family in
the Liverpool cellar presents social evil. The incident
follows the scene in the graveyard and dead-house, where
the buried are trampled under the feet of the living, and
the unburied cadavers, scavenged by down-and-outs, are
morbidly exposed. The wrecked oblivious dead, juxtaposed with the all-but-oblivious dying, cast on the latter
a peculiar horror of neglect. The burning corpse[10] and
the cholera[11] are equally terrible. The latter is conveyed
in as strong a statement as fiction can offer on the con-
dition of the poor; and though Melville's voyage provided no such episode his imagination seized powerfully
what he had heard (cholera came first in an immigrant
ship from Le Havre the year before *Redburn* was written).
The former episode, whether Melville observed it or
recorded a fo'c'sle story, communicates a poetic and
imaginative significance of shock. "He began to make his
particulars so suggestive that they appeared emble-
matic," Leon Howard observes of *White Jacket*, and this
incident in *Redburn* works like a revelation:

The men rushed towards the bunk, Max with the light,
which he held to the man's face. "No, he's not dead,"
he cried, as the yellow flame wavered for a moment at

the seaman's motionless mouth. But hardly had the words escaped when, to the silent horror of all, two threads of greenish fire, like a forked tongue, darted out between the lips, and in a moment the cadaverous face was crawled over by a swarm of wormlike flames. The lamp dropped from the hand of Max, and went out; while covered all over with spires and sparkles of flame, that faintly crackled in the silence, the un-covered parts of the body burned before us, precisely like phosphorescent shark in a midnight sea. The eyes were open and fixed; the mouth was curled like a scroll, and every lean feature firm as in life; while the whole face, now wound in curls of soft blue flame, wore an aspect of grim defiance and eternal death. Prome-theus, blasted by fire on the rock.

One arm, its red shirt-sleeve rolled up, exposed the man's name, tattooed in vermilion, near the hollow of the middle joint; and as if there were something peculiar in the painted flesh, every vibrating letter burned so white that you might read the flaming name in the flickering ground of blue.

Good though *Redburn* is, however, *White Jacket* has a finer force and coherence, a totality outmatching *Red-burn*'s miscellaneous effects. It records the facts of a way of life but it is also a document of superb human quality. At its heart is a passion for autonomy and dignity. From the beginning, through all the afflictions imposed in the name of discipline, Melville makes felt the ignominies which can break men's pride. He admits that training must be effective, and that those whose spirits survive are admirable—"fellows that it does your heart good to look at, hearty old members of the Old Guard." He prizes courage—"as with ships, so with men; he who turns his back to the foe gives him an advantage. Whereas, our ribbed chests, like the ribbed bows of a frigate, are as bulkheads to dam off an onset." But if manliness is tough, senseless severities are hideous, and denouncing "obsolete barbarism" he has a radical strength which brings Cobbett to mind:

Irrespective of incidental considerations, we assert that flogging in the Navy is opposed to the essential dignity of man, which no legislator has a right to violate; that it is oppressive, and glaringly unequal in its operations; that it is utterly repugnant to the spirit of our democratic institutions; indeed, that it involves a lingering trait of the worst times of a barbarous feudal aristocracy; in a word, we denounce it as religiously, morally, and immutably *wrong*.[12]

Protest is, however, only one element. Between the opening light-hearted extravagance (light-heartedness to avert self-pity; as Dana observes, "Whatever your feelings may be, you must make a joke of everything at sea; and if you were to fall from aloft and be caught in the belly of a sail, and thus saved from instant death, it would not do to look at all disturbed")—between this and the final note of moral autonomy and noble endurance there lies a whole world of social culture. The presiding genius is Smollett's, in the sharp detail, the uncompromising force, the unsqueamishness. But though he and Lesage are referred to ("What a debt do we owe you!" Melville had exclaimed in *Omoo*, finding Smollett's novels out in Polynesia), and though "Cadwallader Cuticle, M.D." out-Smolletts Smollett himself, the derivation is less individual than from a whole nautical tradition. The sailors' skills, pastimes, crafts, songs, customs, superstitions, and argot add up to a world with something of myth about it, real yet touched by fantasy, with a full flavour as though individual perception were crossed by folk memory. The persons are lifelike and something more, and the incidents have a compelling, accentuated quality such as marks the whole admirable chapter on "The Good or Bad Temper of Men-of-War's

Men," or that on "General Training in a Man-of-War."

Melville compressed the events of fourteen months into the shorter period of the homeward voyage from Callao; his use of his material, firsthand or hearsay, is thoroughly examined in Charles R. Anderson's *Melville in the South Seas*, which identifies Claret, Mad Jack, Shenly, Lemsford, and others. Melville himself shrank, he told Dana, from "anything that approaches to a personal identification . . . with characters that were only intended to furnish samples of a tribe."[13] But the modern reader can observe the identifications and yet take the book generically. Two points on which he may be curious is how far Jack Chase and Cuticle are authentic. Chase was certainly real, and *Billy Budd* is dedicated to him. Several of his exploits in the novel are matters of record, and, idealised though he must seem, Melville presumably did not in this case really falsify the actuality he so well serves elsewhere. As for Cuticle, he is equally certainly fictitious, and decidedly not Surgeon-of-the-Fleet William Johnson; so much must be said in justice. His operation[14] presumably germinated from the episode of Jack Rattlin's broken leg in *Roderick Random*. Melville, of course, invents or imports a good deal; a shipmate, Harrison Robertson the captain's clerk, noted in his copy of the book,

> Some of the incidents & characters described in this book, occurred on board the Frigate "United States" —in which I returned home, via Cape Horn, in 1844. Other incidents described are either purely imaginary, or happened at some other time & place—The author probably has made his book, not from personal experience wholly, but has patched together scraps picked up from some other person's journal, or conversation—Most of the characters & incidents described are grossly caricatured, or exaggerated.[15]

To mention some of Melville's additions will indicate

the enrichment he introduces. They include the comedy
of the grog failure;[16] the theatricals;[17] the amputation;[18]
the "massacre of the beards"[19] (historical, but effected
before Melville joined the ship); the consequent flogging
of Old Ushant (the terrible account of flogging through
the fleet seems to derive from Samuel Leech's *Thirty
Years from Home*, 1843); and above all White Jacket's
near-flogging[20] and his fall from the yard-arm.[21] Some
of these episodes are the natural stuff of sailors' yarns,
but some are much more. Even Smollett does not equal
the comedy and horror of Cuticle's surgery, in the force
and precision of shock that Melville achieves, the bril-
liantly controlled violence. Stylised as intense caricature
the scene is bearable, just: the quality of the writing enables one to hold just adequately at bay the sensory
revulsion, hypnotised by the exactitude of effect, braced
by the severity of the comedy. Given that Melville saw
no such scene (and the ship's records mention none), the
vividness of the following, in which Cuticle is demon-
strating his celerity, is beyond praise:

"Stand by, now, you messmates; keep hold of his arms;
pin him down. Steward, put your hand on the artery;
I shall commence as soon as his pulse begins to—*now,
now!*" Letting fall the wrist, feeling the thigh carefully,
and bowing over it in an instant, he drew the fatal
knife unerringly across the flesh. As it first touched the
part, the row of surgeons simultaneously dropped their
eyes to the watches in their hands, while the patient
lay, with eyes horribly distended, in a kind of waking
trance. Not a breath was heard; but as the quivering
flesh parted in a long, lingering gash, a spring of blood
welled up between the living walls of the wound, and
two thick streams, in opposite directions, coursed down
the thigh. The sponges were instantly dipped in the
purple pool; every face present was pinched to a point
with suspense; the limb writhed; the man shrieked;

his messmates pinioned him; while round and round
the leg went the unpitying cut.

"The saw!" said Cuticle.

Instantly it was in his hand.

Full of the operation, he was about to apply it,
when, looking up, and turning to the assistant surgeons,
he said, "Would any of you young gentlemen like to
apply the saw? A splendid subject!"

Several volunteered; when, selecting one, Cuticle
surrendered the instrument to him, saying, "Don't be
hurried now; be steady."

While the rest of the assistants looked upon their
comrade with glances of envy, he went rather timidly
to work; and Cuticle, who was earnestly regarding him,
suddenly snatched the saw from his hand. "Away,
butcher! you disgrace the profession. Look at *me*!"

For a few minutes the thrilling rasping sound was
heard; and then the topman seemed parted in twain
at the hip, as the leg slowly slid into the arms of the
pale, gaunt man in the shroud, who at once made
away with it, and tucked it out of sight under one of
the guns.[22]

This transfixes one because of the timing and precision.
But a second fictitious scene, White Jacket's arraignment
at the mast, is different, like a realistic nightmare;
William Plomer aptly compares it with Dostoevsky's
sham execution, though there is no sham intention about
this. A horror of flogging has accumulated through the
book (163 men were flogged during Melville's fourteen
months on the *United States*); White Jacket, as yet un-
flogged, has a special loathing of the unexperienced
torture; and finally, the sentence is wholly unjust. The
incident, while purely imaginary, mobilises two powerful though contrasting aspects of Melville's sense of
integrity—the feeling that his inner sovereignty of nature
is inviolable, the feeling, on the other hand, of outrage at

degradation. If any incident focuses the book's central themes, it is this—the themes of arbitrary judgment, tyrannous rank, man's tenacity of life and his right of revolt (even by murder), underdog loyalty, and the chanciness of fate. This last is natural to a book reflecting on adventure and accident, where "Life comes in at one gangway and Death goes overboard at the other," where a sailor on a venial escapade is mortally shot so that over the once-stalwart man ("an arm like a royal-mast and a thigh like a windlass") the wizened Cuticle can stand wielding his knife. And here, save for an unprecedented intervention from the lower deck, the unguilty White Jacket would become a murderer, and Claret be flung from his command to death in the sea.

The third major importation, the yard-arm fall, comes from Nathaniel Ames's *Mariner's Sketches* (1830). Since Ames is hard to come by, and space prohibits the reprinting of both long passages for collation, it seems best to reproduce Ames and give the reader his own chance of comparison. Ames is effective, but Melville's reworking is on a different level of literary quality. Here is Ames, when he finds himself falling:

My first sensation was surprise; I could not imagine where I was, but soon ascertained from the rushing of the air by my ears that I was falling, and that head foremost. . . . In an instant the recollection came into my head that one of the quarter-deck guns was directly under me, and I should in all human probability be dashed in pieces upon it. I would have given the world to vent my feelings in cries. . . . All this while there was a blood red light before my eyes, through which a thousand horrible forms were constantly gliding. Then I thought of home, and the forms of all I hold dear on earth, and many others. . . . Then the recollection of the infernal gun and the consequent smash across the breech of it put all these phantoms to flight, and I felt that peculiar sickness and distress at the stomach, which it is said one experiences when one is at the point of undergoing a sudden and violent death. . . .

But no words can express my delight, my extacy, at finding myself *overboard*, instead of on the gun. I kept going down, down, till it appeared to me that the seven fathoms and a half (the depth of water at our anchorage) had more than doubled. . . .

After a while I became stationary and soon began slowly to ascend. When I looked up, I saw high, very high above me, a dim greenish light, which became brighter and brighter till at last I bounced on the surface like a cork. I immediately swam to the accommodation ladder and went on board.[23]

The only dubious quality in *White Jacket* is the rhetoric occasioned by Jack Chase. This is a sort of dazzle in the disciple's eyes from the glamour of the noble veteran, or perhaps a kind of code in which Melville renders his affection for a man William Plomer calls "a central figure in the Melvillean mythology."[24] Chase, if too floridly romanticised, is still a heartening presence in the book. His indomitable exuberance counterpoises the harshness, and his extravagance is only an extreme form of the enriching exaggeration which raises the book above realism into a kind of fable, a fully-elicited rendering of life in significant relationships of history and tradition, evil and good, discipline and danger, animal doggedness and spiritual autonomy, daily intimacy and oceanic largeness, existence interlinked (none more so) yet individualistic, a life hierarchically ranked (with the officers "shipping their quarter-deck faces") yet, as Jack Chase observes, "the thing to bring us mortals out." The rhapsodic strain is not without value in its exultance. By turns Melville manages the mock-heroic of nautical yarning, a fullness and often a sensitiveness of effect, unflagging energy of style, and indeed beauty and nobility, a foretaste in clean gravity of *Billy Budd*. And at the least he never fails to be interesting.

REFERENCES

1. *M.*, ch. clxxxi (st. ed., II. 340).
2. *Letters*, pp. 85–6.
3. *Letters*, p. 91.
4. *Letters*, p. 106.
5. *R.*, ch. xiii.
6. *R.*, ch. iv.
7. *R.*, ch. xxviii.
8. *R.*, chs. xxxii–xli.
9. *R.*, ch. xxii.
10. *R.*, ch. xlviii.
11. *R.*, ch. lviii.
12. *W.J.*, ch. xxxv.
13. *Letters*, p. 107.
14. *W.J.*, ch. lxiii.
15. Charles R. Anderson, *Melville in the South Seas*, 1939, p. 395.
16. *W.J.*, chs. xiv, xxxvii.
17. *W.J.*, ch. xxiii.
18. *W.J.*, chs. lxi–iii.
19. *W.J.*, ch. lxxxv.
20. *W.J.*, ch. lxvii.
21. *W.J.*, ch. xcii.
22. *W.J.*, ch. lxiii.
23. Nathaniel Ames, *A Mariner's Sketches*, 1830, pp. 227–9.
24. *W.J.*, intro. William Plomer, Chiltern Library, 1952, p. ix.

CHAPTER V

MOBY DICK

Moby Dick was written under the pressure of the intense development Melville described to Hawthorne in June 1851, when the book was nearing completion.[1] It was written, too, under other stresses. "The calm, the coolness, the silent grass-growing mood in which a man *ought* always to compose,—that, I fear, can seldom be mine," he protested. "Dollars damn me; and the malicious Devil is forever grinning in upon me, holding the door ajar."[2] But the main stress seems to have been one which took him off his guard, as the impulses of *Mardi* had done, the sense of a vast unforeseeable creativity which committed him to an exploration of almost unnerving hazards. The account of Pierre's authorship[3] seems to reflect, not the less revealingly for the touches of mockery, what must have been Melville's experience with his own preceding novel. In effect it is Lombardo's situation over again with his "Koztanza" (Melville's own situation with *Mardi*), but repeated at a different level of intensity and with a far deeper sense of spiritual danger, if of exhilaration too. Driven by "the burning desire to deliver what he thought to be new" (and also by the prospect of being penniless), Pierre pours all his knowledge ("his multifarious, incidental, bibliographic encounterings") into the original depth of his own mind and experience ("that bottomless spring of original thought which the occasion and time had caused to burst out in himself"). He finds himself inescapably committed to an unprecedented spiritual exploration, as if of mountains revealed "peak crowded on peak, and spur sloping on spur, and chain

D

jammed behind chain." Did not the revelation come by
degrees, it would overwhelm the power to endure it:

> Only by judicious degrees appointed of God does man
> come at last to gain his Mont Blanc and take an over-
> topping view of those Alps; and even then the tithe is
> not known; and far over the invisible Atlantic, the
> Rocky Mountains and the Andes are yet unbeheld.
> Appalling is the soul of a man! Better might one be
> pushed off into the material spaces beyond the utter-
> most orbit of our sun, than once feel himself fairly
> afloat in himself.

Later in *Pierre* the process of composition is described as
hysterically desperate,[4] but one need not read too much
of this back into *Pierre*'s precursor. The letter to Hawthorne also offers signs of desperation, it is true, but with
a gusty humour quite foreign to Pierre's case, though
quite consonant with much of *Moby Dick*.

The crisis around 1850, whatever the cause, involved
his passionate recognition of the tragic sense of life—the
"tragicalness of human thought in its own unbiased,
native, and profounder workings."[5] The mood is that of
Yeats's aphorism, "We begin to live when we have conceived life as tragedy." Or, as Babbalanja had put it,
"He knows himself, and all that's in him, who knows
adversity."[6] To say this is not to forget (nor should it
ever be forgotten, otherwise the balance of the book goes
wrong) that *Moby Dick* contains large and strong elements of the comic (so indeed does *Pierre*, though less
effective); the book's controlling theme is the interrela-
tion of the dark and the light. But the powerful new
impulse is to recognise tragic mystery. It was doubtless reflected in the metaphysical talks recorded in the 1849–50
journal; it is certainly reflected in the passages Melville
marked in Elizabethan playwrights, and especially in the
Shakespeare he took avidly to reading in 1849, passages
on the treacherousness of man, man's ambiguous place

in the universe, the inscrutability of God, and other moral-metaphysical dilemmas. The *Inferno* (he bought a Dante in 1848) and *Hamlet* are much invoked among the dark bewilderments of *Pierre*; Montaigne influenced his sceptical enquiries; and in the Bible and Seneca he marked with strong endorsements passages on the autonomy man wins through adversity.

But the main literary precipitant was Hawthorne. The crucial passages of Melville's articles on "Hawthorne and his Mosses" are wholly relevant to Melville himself, and his sense of a kindred spirit accompanied him from the early stages of *Moby Dick* and through the wonderful letters he wrote Hawthorne during composition and after publication. What Melville perceives in Hawthorne, one deduces from the rapture with which he hails it, is a version of himself:

Spite of all the Indian-summer sunlight on the hither side of Hawthorne's soul, the other side—like the dark half of the physical sphere—is shrouded in a blackness, ten times black. But this blackness but gives more effect to the ever-moving dawn, that forever advances through it, and circumnavigates his world. Whether Hawthorne has simply availed himself of this mystical blackness as a means to the wondrous effects he makes it to produce in his lights and shades; or whether there really lurks in him, perhaps unknown to himself, a touch of Puritanic gloom,—this I cannot altogether tell. Certain it is, however, that this great power of blackness in him derives its force from its appeals to that Calvinistic sense of Innate Depravity and Original Sin, from whose visitations, in some shape or other, no deeply thinking mind is always and wholly free. For, in certain moods, no man can weigh this world without throwing in something, somehow like Original Sin, to strike the uneven balance. . . . You may be witched by his sunlight—transported by the bright gildings in the

skies he builds over you; but there is the blackness of
darkness beyond; and even his bright gildings but
fringe and play upon the edges of thunder-clouds. . . .

Now it is that blackness in Hawthorne, of which I
have spoken, that so fixes and fascinates me. It may be,
nevertheless, that it is too largely developed in him.
Perhaps he does not give us a ray of light for every shade
of his dark. But however this may be, this blackness it is
that furnishes the infinite obscure of his background—
that background against which Shakespeare plays his
grandest conceits. . . . Nor need you fix upon that
blackness in him [Hawthorne], if it suit you not. Nor,
indeed, will all readers discern it; for it is, mostly,
insinuated to those who may best understand it and
account for it; it is not obtruded upon everyone alike.[7]

" Shakespeare," he adds, "has been approached." This
double sense that darkness has the profounder truth, but
that dark and light must be known together, that both
in due (though not equal) proportions are indispensable
parts of wisdom, is the message of that astonishing
chapter in *Moby Dick* on the try-works.[8] The midnight
fire scene lures Ishmael into a tranced vision of Hell,
during which he unwittingly reverses his sense of direction, facing away from the compass (he is helmsman) and
seeing only darkness, and the ship apparently leaving all
havens behind rather than seeking any ahead. He reads
the symbolism; do not gaze into Hell too long; do not
lose the tiller and compass; believe the illumination of
the natural sun and not the nightmare distortions of
"artificial fire" (Ahab's frenzy). But though Ahab's frenzy
be "unnatural hallucination," even the natural truth
of sunlight includes the dark as well as the bright—"The
sun hides not the ocean, which is the dark side of this
earth, and which is two-thirds of this earth. So, therefore,
that mortal man who hath more of joy than sorrow in
him, that mortal man cannot be true."[9] The tragic pre-

ponderates but—and this is the grand poise of *Moby
Dick*—this preponderance does not invalidate joy, does
not authorise despair. In "The Encantadas" he was to
express this again:

> Tortoises as well as turtles are of such a make, that if
> you but put them on their backs you thereby expose
> their bright sides without the possibility of their re-
> covering themselves, and turning into view the other.
> But after you have done this, and because you have done
> this, you should not swear that the tortoise has no dark
> side. . . . Neither should he, who cannot turn the tor-
> toise from its natural position so as to hide the darker
> and expose his livelier aspect, like a great October
> pumpkin in the sun, for that cause declare the creature
> to be one total inky blot. The tortoise is both black and
> bright.[10]

"There is a wisdom that is woe; but there is a woe that
is madness"—that is the sane moral of the try-works
episode. Ahab, then, though greater than his crew,
blasphemes against life in the degree and nature of his
blackness. The balance, it seems, is to recognise as Hawthorne did the "power of blackness," without denying
the "ever-moving dawn," to acknowledge man's pro-
clivity to sin (so stressed in New England Calvinism)
while admitting (though not over-rating) the "bright
gildings."

Fixed and fascinated by Hawthorne's blackness, Melville, who in *Mardi* had converted Babbalanja to a Christian ethic, and in *White Jacket* had foreseen "some
blessed placid haven, however remote at present" as the
destination of his world-frigate, commits himself to a
heroic plunge. With abundant comedy still to vindicate
the "gildings," with ultimate moral sanity and spiritual
resilience, he nevertheless reads the world as a con-
dominium of good and evil, with evil the weightier
power and emotionally the more engrossing. And in the

excitement of this commitment, of the wholeheartedness
with which he expresses Ahab's belief in ultimate malice,
he tells Hawthorne that "[*Moby Dick's*] motto (the secret
one) [is] Ego non baptiso te in nomine—but make out
the rest yourself."[11] The words omitted—"patris, sed in
nomine diaboli"—are those Ahab uses when baptising
his harpoon in the blood of the pagan harpooners.[12]

With an emotional commitment, then, on one side to
the excitements of blackness, and on the other to moral
enlightenment, the book finds its moral and metaphysical
dynamic in the interplay of opposing principles, con-
fused together though they often are, and in the rejection
of any such optimistic monopsychism as is represented by
Emerson's "eternal ONE—this deep power in which we
exist, and whose beatitude is all accessible to us, . . .
self-sufficing and perfect in every hour,"[13] or his "bene-
ficent purpose [which] lies in wait for us," so that "if . . .
we feel that the soul [of Nature] streams through us, we
shall find the peace of the morning dwelling first in our
hearts."[14] To this, and perhaps to Thoreau too, Melville
provides his answer in *Pierre*:

> Say what some poets will, Nature is not so much her
> own ever-sweet interpreter, as the mere supplier of that
> cunning alphabet whereby, selecting and combining as
> he pleases, each man reads his own peculiar lesson
> according to his own peculiar mind and mood.[15]

This ambiguity of Nature's evidence, this wide liberty of
interpreting, adds greatly to the richness of *Moby Dick*,
for each character's life is his own stream of consciousness
and each man reads each event "according to his own
peculiar mind and mood." The book and the symbols in
it are composites of individual readings. Melville's experience in writing it seems to have been a reading of the
"alphabet" in an extraordinary access of spiritual ven-
turesomeness. *Mardi* had been venturesome but not (save
in so far as Lombardo reflects such a thing) with the

"appalling" sense of a man thus unreservedly "afloat in himself." This new sense of "the intrepid effort of the soul to keep the open independence of her sea" charges the symbolic figure of Bulkington here with passionate rhetoric, as it does the symbolic story of Pierre later.

Moby Dick, then, Melville wrote to Sarah Morewood, "is by no means the sort of book for you. It is not a piece of fine feminine Spitalfields silk—but is of the horrible texture of a fabric that should be woven of ship's cables and hawsers. A Polar wind blows through it, & birds of prey hover over it."[16] Answering a "joy-giving and exultation-breeding letter" from Hawthorne (not, alas, extant), he made the famous comment that "a sense of unspeakable security is in me this moment, on account of your having understood the book. I have written a wicked book, and feel spotless as the lamb."[17] "Wicked" presumably reflects the blasphemous imaginations embodied in Ahab, the "grand, ungodly, godlike man," "alien . . . to the census of Christendom," "nor gods nor men his neighbours," with the "prophetic" name of the Old Testament warrior who did evil in the sight of the Lord above all that were before him. Mrs Morewood told George Duyckinck in December 1851 that Melville was "a pleasant companion at all times" but sadly prone to irreverence.[18] The irreverence could be skittish: it could also be bold, deep, and troubled.

It will be necessary later to explain how Melville conducts his moral exploration through his narrative and symbols, and this, being a complex matter, cannot be done briefly; in Melville criticism, symbol-interpreting is apt to crowd everything else out of the nest altogether. At the head of any treatment of *Moby Dick*, therefore, there needs to be proclaimed its grandeur as narrative, and the marvellous power of its writing. In their sheer importance these things should have the major space, and they would receive it were they not so evident that no reader can fail to observe for himself the extraordinary breadth and imaginativeness of context in which Melville presents "the overwhelming idea of the great whale," and the human history and enterprise that go with it, or the poetic power of the writing which conveys so wide a range of the subject's significances.

The treatment of the material, "worked up by a romancer,"[19] reflects Melville's interests in romantic fiction and Jacobean drama. Scott and Cooper in particular had established the supremacy of the romance, the story akin to poetry or myth, dealing not with daily realism so much as with the excitingly unusual. Told that his Indians were not "real," Cooper replied that his aim was "to present the *beau-idéal* of their characters," and the *Knickerbocker Magazine* praised him for the element of enthusiastic fancy—"He was called upon first to drive away the atmosphere of familiarity that surrounded and degraded the landscape, and then to breathe through all the region from his own resources of fancy and feeling the roseate air of romance."[20] That general intention, though less roseate, combined in Melville with admiration for the attitudes of the Byronic hero and the styles of Jacobean playwrights, to produce impassioned rhetoric, clashes of character external and internal, daring of imagination, and dramatic devices like soliloquies and stage-directions or stylised and expressionist dialogue-fantasy. In other words, the novel is conceived as much in terms of poetry and drama as of prose; it differs in this respect (though not in all others) from, say, *White Jacket* which so recently preceded it. Some of the results are glaring enough and must be recognised—faults of stagyness, melodramatic excess, mystery-mongering (Fedallah's crew, for instance), and significances over-insisted upon ("The Whiteness of the Whale," or Pip's babblings). (The unreliable melodramatics unwittingly parody themselves in " 'Ready!' was the half-hissed reply";[21] which half? one wonders.) But blemishes, many though they are, are wholly outweighed by the fine things, and indeed in a way, even in their fulsomeness, are correlative with the fine things, signs of a very rich and abundant manner. The things Melville enjoys doing and does well are legion—the Dickensian picturesque of the Spouter Inn, the comedy of Bildad and Peleg, the strange reverence of Queequeg's Ramadan, the sailor-yarning (Ishmael in New Bedford, the *Town-Ho*'s story, the meeting with the *Rosebud*, and so on), Father Mapple's chapel and sermon, the splendid accounts of whaling processes, Queequeg's rescue of Tashtego, Stubb's pitch-poling, and always the wonderful sense of how a scene should go, notably exemplified in the constituents of the "Mat-Maker" chapter[22] (sultry afternoon, whale-shout, the Malay apparitions—the dramatic timing is skilful), or the try-works scene,[23] or the Candles,[24] or, invariably, the hunting and the appearances of the whales. The finest scenes are those, by and large, which Melville leaves to make their own effect without his moralising—those like "the first lowering,"[25] the sighting of the great squid,[26] the whale-killings,[27] and the finest thing of all, the grand armada of whales with the whale-nursery at its heart.[28]

The writing is frequently overcharged; words like "devilish," "remorseless," "appalling," and "ghastly" can be collected by the hundred, for too often Melville must not only do the reader's work for him but make him feel he is responding tremendously in taking in so many superlative emotions. The results can on occasion be very bad indeed. But the fact remains that over a wide range of qualities, from the sound prose of the naturalist (though never for long without a felicity inaccessible to most naturalists) to the most unabashedly grandiose, Melville unfolds a masterly power of style. Its most evident quality is fullness of effect. Nothing is without body or flavour, from the simple appreciative vigour of phrases like "a brown and brawny company with bosky beards" to the easy precision of "a long living arc of a leap", or the rich equivalence of sound and sense in "the measureless crush and crash of the sperm whale's ponderous flukes," or "a mighty volition of ungraduated, instantaneous swiftness," or the auditory expressiveness (with the admirable "collapsed") of the last chapter's last sentence—"Now small fowls flew screaming over the yet yawning gulf; a sullen white surf beat against its steep sides; then all collapsed, and the great shroud of the sea rolled on as it rolled five thousand years ago." The subtle and wonderful music can be represented by the passage on the moonlit spirit-spout—

> It was while gliding through these latter waters that one serene and moonlight night, when all the waves rolled by like scrolls of silver; and, by their soft, suffused seethings, made what seemed a silvery silence, not a solitude; on such a silent night a silvery jet was seen far in advance of the white bubbles at the bow. Lit up by the moon, it looked celestial; seemed some plumed and glittering god uprising from the sea.[29]

And who could fault a sentence like that which describes Moby Dick's placid motion?—"Behind, the blue waters interchangeably flowed over into the moving valley of his steady wake; and on either hand bright bubbles arose and danced by his side."[30]

The nonchalance with which Melville can achieve an effect of untroubled grandeur is a good illustration of Keats's "Might half-slumbering on his own right arm"— in, for example, "Presently, as we thus glided in chase, the monster perpendicularly flitted his tail forty feet into the air, and then sank out of sight like a tower swallowed up."[31] The sharpness of registration already evident in *White Jacket* reappears, perfected with an uncanny sense of timing, in scenes like (though no other scene is quite like) the fatality of Ahab:

> The harpoon was darted; the stricken whale flew forward; with igniting velocity the line ran through the groove; ran foul. Ahab stooped to clear it; he did clear

it; but the flying turn caught him by the neck, and voicelessly as Turkish mutes bowstring their victim, he was shot out of the boat, ere the crew knew he was gone. Next instant, the heavy eyesplice in the rope's final end flew out of the stark-empty tub, knocked down an oarsman, and smiting the sea, disappeared in its depths.[32]

Seeking a single example of Melville at his most moving, one is inevitably drawn to the whale-nursery surrounded by the distracted school, in "The Grand Armada." As Augustine Birrell once observed, "to be really eloquent in cold print requires great courage." Melville is eloquent, but his eloquence serves the beauty of his subject:

When at last the jerking harpoon drew out, and the towing whale sideways vanished; then, with the taper-ing force of his parting commotion, we glided between two whales into the innermost heart of the shoal, as if from some mountain torrent we had slid into a serene valley lake. Here the storms in the roaring glens be-tween the outermost whales were heard but not felt. In this central expanse the sea presented that smooth satin-like surface, called a sleek, produced by the subtle moisture thrown off by the whale in his more quiet moods. Yes, we were now in that enchanted calm which they say lurks at the heart of every commotion. And still in the distracted distance we beheld the tumults of the outer concentric circles, and saw successive pods of whales, eight or ten in each, swiftly going round and round, like multiplied spans of horses in a ring; and so closely shoulder to shoulder, that a Titanic circus-rider might easily have overarched the middle ones, and so have gone round on their backs. . . .

But far beneath this wondrous world upon the sur-face, another and still stranger world met our eyes as we gazed over the side. For, suspended in those watery vaults, floated the forms of the nursing mothers of the

whales, and those that by their enormous girth seemed
shortly to become mothers. The lake, as I have hinted,
was to a considerable depth exceedingly transparent;
and as human infants while suckling will calmly and
fixedly gaze away from the breast, as if leading two
different lives at the time; and while yet drawing mortal nourishment, be still spiritually feasting upon some
unearthly reminiscence;—even so did the young of
these whales seem looking up towards us, but not at us,
as if we were but a bit of Gulfweed in their new-born
sight. Floating on their sides, the mothers also seemed
quietly eyeing us. One of these little infants, that from
certain queer tokens seemed hardly a day old, might
have measured some fourteen feet in length, and some
six feet in girth. He was a little frisky; though his body
seemed scarce yet recovered from that irksome position
it had so lately occupied in the maternal reticule;
where, tail to head, and all ready for the final spring,
the unborn whale lies bent like a Tartar's bow. The
delicate side-fins, and the palms of his flukes, still
freshly retained the plaited crumpled appearance of a
baby's ears newly arrived from foreign parts.[33]

The powers there revealed, ample, disciplined, eloquent,
sensitive, imaginative and reverent, show Melville at his
best; the passage is individually fine, but, more than that,
it expresses the book's central sense of creativity. That
that achievement, if the best of its kind, is only one
among a range of kinds which rise to equal heights in
varieties of power and manner is the measure of Melville's
accomplishment in the writing of *Moby Dick*.

If his reading of Hawthorne precipitated his sense of the
tragic, his reading of Carlyle, and probably of Emerson
too, precipitated important elements of style and method.
While *Moby Dick* was under way he was reading *Sartor
Resartus*, and Carlyle's Teufelsdröckh, "Professor of
Things in General," given to a "high, silent, meditative

Transcendentalism" (not that Melville's was silent, however), virtually prefigures Melville himself. The account of Teufelsdröckh's style reads like a review of *Moby Dick*:

> we find consummate vigour, a true inspiration; his burning Thoughts step forth in fit burning Words, like so many full-formed Minervas, issuing amid flame and splendour from Jove's head; a rich, idiomatic diction, picturesque allusions, fiery poetic emphasis, or quaint tricksy turns; all the graces and terrors of a wild Imagination. . . . A wild tone pervades the whole utterance of the man . . . now screwing itself aloft as into the Song of Spirits, or else the shrill mockery of Fiends; now sinking in cadences, not without melodious heartiness, though sometimes abrupt enough, into the common pitch.[34]

Reviewers had detected, and deplored, Carlyle's influence in *Mardi* and *White Jacket*, and Evert Duyckinck was to deplore it likewise in *Moby Dick*. Melville is abnormally, and often damagingly, susceptible to other manners and ideas, undergoing infections one after another; his "machinery for exploring an unknown situation" is to try everything that excites him, to let the "certain something unmanageable" have its head. But in *Moby Dick* the styles thus produced have great character and are, in general (though one can find some reckless extravagances), integrated to great effects, like the artificial styles of Jacobean drama or Milton's epics. Carlyle affected the rhetorical patterns, the dramatic accentuations, the dogmatic address, but more importantly he, with Hawthorne and Emerson, encouraged the discovery of analogical significances and symbolical meanings. Something must now be said about these devices.

Carlyle's, or Teufelsdröckh's, forceful, rhapsodical, and complicated style, his analogy-mongering, and his omniscience in reference ("walking by the light of Oriental, Pelasgic, Scandinavian, Egyptian, Otaheitean,

Ancient and Modern researches of every conceivable kind")[35] pointed the way Melville wished to go, particularly in placing man "in the centre of Immensities, in the conflux of Eternities."[36] "Man," Carlyle wrote, "though . . . based on the small Visible does nevertheless extend down to the infinite Deeps of the Invisible"[37] and all that surrounds him is symbolic of this Invisible:

> The thing Visible, nay the thing Imagined, the thing in any way conceived of as Visible, what is it but a Garment, a Clothing of the higher, celestial Invisible? . . . All visible things are emblems; what thou seest is not there on its own account. . . . Matter exists only spiritually, and to represent some Idea, and body it forth.[38]

That passage is virtually reproduced in Ahab's outburst when Starbuck reproves him for seeking "vengeance on a dumb brute"—

> All visible objects, man, are but as pasteboard masks. But in each event—in the living act, the undoubted deed—there, some unknown but still reasoning thing puts forth the mouldings of its features from behind the unreasoning mask.[39]

As for Emerson, though Melville derided his bland evasions of the reality of evil, he admired him as a "thought-diver."[40] (Teufelsdröckh's volume, one recalls, is "a very Sea of Thought . . . wherein the toughest pearl-diver may dive to his utmost strength and return not only with sea-wreck but with true orients.")[41] Emerson's belief in patterns and interrelationships ("Polarity, or action and reaction, we meet in every part of Nature")[42] pervades Melville's technique of correspondences; and Melville's processes of thought, restlessly speculative in divining metaphysical significances, are transcendental though not optimistic attempts to "strike through the mask." From his first novel he had worked

from fact to larger meanings. In *Moby Dick*, while he
defends its factual reality, and denies that Moby Dick
(the whale, not the novel) is "a monstrous fable ... a
hideous and intolerable allegory," he uses the whale in
its majesty, dangerousness, valuableness, and the varied
emotions its pursuers feel, as his means of examining
"this great allegory—the world."[43]

The interpenetration of nature and supernature is
taken for granted in the New England tradition: in his
story "The Lightning-Rod Man" Melville was to borrow,
and defiantly satirise, the theme from Cotton Mather's
Magnalia Christi Americana that the thunder-stroke is
God's wrath. Melville parodies this interpenetration in the
splendidly funny scenes of Bildad's exhortations ("Don't
whale it too much a' the Lord's Day, men; but don't miss
a fair chance either, that's rejecting Heaven's good gifts,"
and so on) but it is fundamental to his conceptions. As
Yvor Winters puts it, and as one knows in Hawthorne:

> The fusion of the physical with the spiritual in New
> England is older than Melville; the New Englanders of
> whom Melville wrote were descended from the Mathers
> and their townsmen, from the contemporaries of the
> more recent Jonathan Edwards, men who saw chimneys
> suddenly leap into flame in the midst of a revival sermon,
> upon whom a church might fall immediately following
> a preacher's prophecy of doom. With physical and
> spiritual adventure alike, and with the two interpene-
> trative, the New Englanders were familiar from child-
> hood.[44]

By literary fashion, natural disposition, and native tradition, Melville was ready to follow Hawthorne in using
fiction as parable and to outgo him in mobilising the
whole world of mind and nature; his reading of life, like
Carlyle's and Emerson's, takes the interdependence of all
phenomena as the clue to metaphysical purpose. "O
Nature, and O soul of man! how far beyond all utterance

are your linked analogies! not the smallest atom stirs or
lives on matter, but has its cunning duplicate in mind."[45]
But unlike Emerson, he sees this interdependence in
terms not of a harmonious whole but of interplay between
aspects of a Manichaean division.

Nature being, as Carlyle said, "written in all colours
and motions, uttered in all tones of jubilee and wail"
(though hardly also, as he, Emerson, and Thoreau said
it was, "harmonious"), Melville rivals his and Emerson's
virtuosity in indicating relationships of paradox, comparison, antithesis, interminglings or separations of calm
and storm, safety and danger, comedy and terror, darkness and light, land and sea, love and hate, the quotidian
and the transcendent; one would think he had Emerson's
"Compensation" by heart. Thematic echoes and juxta-
positions abound. "There is no quality in this world that
is not what it is merely by contrast. Nothing exists in
itself"—this jocose assertion about a warm blanket in a
cold bedroom applies throughout, though "interaction"
would apply better than "contrast." So the Quaker
whalers are "the most sanguinary of all sailors . . .
Quakers with a vengeance"; Christian Ishmael dis-
covers from Polynesian Queequeg the equivalence of
faiths, pagan or Presbyterian; men and animals are all
hunters and hunted ("all killers, on land and on sea;
Bonapartes and Sharks included");[46] Platonic musings
on the "deep, blue, bottomless soul pervading mankind
and nature"[47] can end in violent physical death; a
wrecked crew swim in "serene, exasperating sunlight,
that smiled on as if at a birth or burial";[48] "the most
fragrant ambergris [is] found in the heart of decay";[49]
the folds of the sinking *Pequod*'s flag "calmly undulated,
with ironical coincidings, over the destroying billows
they almost touched."[50] This can be wilful, obtrusive,
tiresome. But as the chapter-title "The Symphony" suggests, Melville wanted something that music might
provide—themes, echoes, related or contrasted keys.

How far deliberately and how far by instinctive organisation of innumerable elements it is impossible to say, but
the book is admirably ordered, from the rueful-comic
opening, crossed with "the overwhelming idea of the
great whale" and the "everlasting itch for things remote,"
to the compelling close, imagined with a force and
strangeness to which it is hard to find a parallel, and then
quietly distanced by the coda of the Epilogue. It is not
that everything falls into a predestined place (the book
has not that kind of contrived order), but that there is a
perpetual richness of material presented in many interesting tones and manners; this whaling voyage is not only
higher and more philosophical than any whaling voyage
ever was, it is broader and more voluminous in effect
likewise. As Willard Thorp observes, "one knows before one has read a half-dozen chapters that one can
trust the amplitude of mind at work here."[51]

It remains now to consider how the moral exploration
takes place, and this means elucidating the symbolism.
Melville of course is more poet than logician; Yvor
Winters not unfairly describes "The Whiteness of the
Whale" as "one of the most appalling specimens of
metaphysical argument in all literature." In general the
symbolism is clear enough, given that its meaning is not
single but reflects the various characters observing it. But
to seek too clear a scheme is to violate the "eternally
unsystematizable." That "potency of life" which Milton
saw in books, "to be as active as that soul was whose
progeny they were," is not helped in the case of *Moby
Dick* by explanation of the kinds all too frequent, eccen-
trically elaborate on one hand, or painstakingly plain
on the other. Much of the meaning introduced itself
subconsciously; this he admits to Sophia Hawthorne:

I had some vague idea while writing it, that the whole
book was susceptible of an allegoric construction, &
also that *parts* of it were—but the speciality of many of

E

the particular subordinate allegories, were [sic] first
revealed to me, after reading Mr Hawthorne's letter,
which, without citing any particular examples, yet
intimated the part-&-parcel allegoricalness of the
whole.[52]

What his allegory is, and is not, is suggested in Stanley
Geist's remark that "all his thought constituted a mode
of perception, all the thought of a philosopher consti-
tutes a reasoned scheme."[53]

Without oversystematising, then, one may examine
certain great components—land, sea, the voyage and
crew, Ahab, Mapple, the Whale, and Ishmael. Each is at
least ambivalent, and the method Melville was to de-
velop in *Pierre*, the exploration of ambiguities, is powerfully present. As Emerson declared, "the wild fertility of
Nature is felt in comparing our rigid names and reputa-
tions with our fluid consciousness";[54] and having felt
this wild fertility in his travelling, his reading, his
speculation, and his own fluid consciousness, Melville
cannot simplify life's complexity under rigid names. So
each thing has more than one significance.

The land is the easiest symbol, the sphere of "safety,
comfort, hearthstone, supper, warm blankets, friends, all
that's kind to our mortalities." Ahab invokes too late
the home ties pressed upon him by the humane Starbuck
which, in his emotion, he wishes to preserve for Starbuck
if not for himself:

Close! stand close to me, Starbuck! let me look into a
human eye; it is better than to gaze into sea or sky;
better than to gaze upon God. By the green land; by
the bright hearthstone! this is the magic glass, man; I
see my wife and my child in thine eye. No, no; stay on
board, on board!—lower not when I do. . . . No, no!
not with the far-away home I see in that eye.[55]

Yet, being the sphere of such things, the land disables
the heroic spirit; the Christian warning that "he that

loveth father or mother more than me is not worthy of me" seems to apply here in a non-Christian way.

The sea is not merely an element to be dared in the course of duty, as it was in *White Jacket* (though it is still merely that to some of the *Pequod*'s men; each man reads each symbol by his own nature). It is the habitat of creatures from the smallest ("brit, the minute yellow substance") to the largest (the great squid's "vast pulpy mass, furlongs in length and breadth"). These creatures exist, innumerable, in the fundamental aspects of activity, passivity, interdependence, "vulturism," procreation, and death; all these the book wonderfully renders. Sea is the sphere of profundity, mystery, danger, and isolation of body and spirit. To face its challenge is obligatory to the heroic nature:

> Glimpses do ye seem to see of that mortally intolerable truth; that all deep, earnest thinking is but the intrepid effort of the soul to keep the open independence of her sea; while the wildest winds of heaven and earth conspire to cast her on the treacherous, slavish shore?[56]

These symbols, it will be seen, are already ambiguous; the land, salvation in one light, is negation in another, and the sea, element of the soul's independence, is also the realm of internecine struggle and the soul's unrest and dread:

> Consider the subtleness of the sea; how its most dreaded creatures glide under water, unapparent for the most part, and treacherously hidden beneath the loveliest tints of azure. Consider also the devilish brilliance and beauty of many of its most remorseless tribes, as the dainty embellished shape of many species of sharks. Consider, once more, the universal cannibalism of the sea; all whose creatures prey upon each other, carrying on eternal war since the world began. Consider all this; and then turn to this green, gentle,

and most docile earth; consider them both, the sea and
the land; and do you not find a strange analogy to
something in yourself? For as this appalling ocean surrounds the verdant land, so in the soul of man there
lies one insular Tahiti, full of peace and joy, but en-
compassed by all the horrors of the half-known life.
God keep thee! Push not off from that isle, thou canst
never return![57]

Such portentousness, one may interpose, is far from being
Melville at his best. The effects are overworked, the
anthropomorphism specious, the address irritating.
These rhapsodic effects ("science tacitly tending towards
the fabulous, normality subtly misshaping itself into
monstrosity,"[58] Richard Chase calls them) are unconvincing. Melville's symbolism is weak when, as often,
the symbolic significances distort the natural phenomena. In fairness, of course, it must be said that if Melville's symbolical enthusiasms sometimes recall the
Carlylean oracular as represented by Miss Toppit in
Martin Chuzzlewit ("Mind and matter glide swift into the
vortex of immensity," and so forth) his actualisations of
natural phenomena are magnificent. Symbolically, at
any rate, the sea is among many other things a challenge
to the spirit to recognise evil, a challenge from which,
once accepted, there is no withdrawing.

What of the voyage and the crew? Compared with
White Jacket, *Moby Dick* marks a vast but not total difference of range. *White Jacket* grew beyond its naturalistic
account of a cruise (in which it would have compared
with, say, Dana's *Two Years before the Mast*) into a symbolic statement about life; the *Neversink*'s homeward
voyage is a test of human behaviour. In the new book this
becomes the *Pequod*'s whaling quest ("by far the longest
of all voyages now or ever made by man")[59] in which,
under one supreme individualist, an assemblage of indi-
vidualists, most symbolically diverse, gathers together for

purposes at one and the same time as material as earning
profits, and as spiritual as challenging the universe's evil.
In this enterprise many impulses combine—Ishmael's
initial misanthropy (comically expressed, but real enough
to make spiritually significant his mellowing into frater-
nity under the generous influence of Queequeg), the
commercialism of Bildad and Peleg, Starbuck's manly
professionalism, Stubbs' "jolly" fatalism, Flask's "ignor-
ant, unconscious fearlessness" in a daily job, and Ahab's
monomania imposing itself on the whole crew, against
Starbuck's half-rebellion and Ishmael's ultimate dis-
engagement. Melville has selected his participants for
representative purposes—Ahab to embody "the general
rage and hate felt by his whole race from Adam down,"
the mates for three natures of obedience and command,
and also as deriving from three centres of the whaling
industry—one a Cape man, one a Nantucketer, one a
Vineyarder. The harpooners are noble savages from
three regions of noble savagery—Daggoo the "imperial
negro," Tashtego the Gayhead-Indian "proud warrior,"
Queequeg the Polynesian prince. Fedallah, doubtless
deriving from the "demon below" who appeared in De
Quincey's Lakeland cottage and became the "fearful
enemy" of his opium-dreams, is a sort of Oriental
Mephistopheles, "some kind of emanation from Ahab
himself," Yvor Winters suggests, "perhaps the sinning
mind as it shows itself distinct from the whole man." And
the *Pequod*'s crew are quite unlike the *Acushnet*'s; they are,
as Melville punningly remarks,

nearly all Islanders in the *Pequod*, *Isolatoes*, too, I call
such, not acknowledging the common continent of
man, but each *Isolato* living on a separate continent of
his own. Yet now, federated along one keel, what a set
these Isolatoes were! An Anacharsis Clootz deputation
from all the isles of the sea, and all the ends of the earth,
accompanying Old Ahab in the *Pequod* to lay the world's

grievances before that bar from which not very many of them ever come back.[60]

This is undisguised paraphrase of Carlyle's *French Revolution*, when, on 19 June 1790, Anacharsis Clootz bursts into the Salle de Manège followed by the most diverse representatives of victimised mankind—

> the Human Species at his heels, Swedes, Spaniards, Polacks; Turks, Chaldeans, Greeks, dwellers in Mesopotamia; behold them all; they have come to claim place in the Grand Federation . . . the mute representatives of their tongue-tied, heavy-laden Nations; Anacharsis and the "Foreigners' Committee" shall have a place at the Federation.

(Melville was to make the same reference in *The Confidence-Man*, and, forty years on, in *Billy Budd* also.) It is not surprising that a crew chosen in this context should second Ahab's self-vindicatory purpose, or that, though they perform real actions (the whaling operations are magnificently convincing), they should symbolise mankind and provide, as in the dance round Pip, a fantasy of cosmopolitan dreams and natures.

Ahab, memorably presented, is next to be assessed—

> He looked like a man cut away from the stake, when the fire has overrunningly wasted all the limbs without consuming them, or taking away one particle from their compacted aged robustness. His whole high, broad form seemed made of solid bronze, and shaped in an unalterable mould, like Cellini's cast Perseus. Threading its way out from among his grey hairs, and continuing right down one side of his tawny scorched face and neck, till it disappeared in his clothing, you saw a slender rod-like mark, lividly whitish. . . . There was an infinity of firmest fortitude, a determinate, unsurrenderable wilfulness, in the fixed and fearless, forward dedication of that glance.[61]

This is the "noble nature" who drives himself to a wreck that carries down not only the *Pequod* but also the symbolic seahawk "from its natural home in the stars," transfixed to the sinking mast, so that the ship, "like Satan, would not sink to hell until she had dragged down a living part of heaven with her."[62] Yet though finally framed in a Satanic context, Ahab starts his voyage on Christmas Day. There is ironic bravado in this, since his motive is to defy whatever gods may be, but with other references (such as his own nails driven into his palms, or the crown of Lombardy he feels himself wearing) it associates him in one particular respect with Christ, that is, as the suffering representative of man. Melville repeatedly links his victimised characters with Christ— Pierre is "Christ-like," the Chola widow, in "The Encantadas," rides on an ass and sees the cross on its shoulders, Billy Budd looks as if crucified, and so on. What this means in Ahab's case is not entirely clear. Partly it is a role Ahab intermittently sees himself in, a part of his subjectivity not to be taken unqualified. Partly, it may be Melville's thrill in being "wicked." Partly, more seriously, it is the sign that Ahab's afflictions are the woe of man taken on the shoulders of one supreme victim. But these significances, present though they are, should not outweigh the major evidence of his fruitless rage and desperate impiety. A comparable ambivalence is already familiar in *Dr Faustus* and *Paradise Lost*.

On the conscious level Melville has gone to great lengths to establish his novel in terms of a relatively orthodox though not specifically Christian morality of humility, charity, and acceptance. Readings which do not observe this make of it something less valuable than it is. They have some excuse, however, for if Melville has tried to preserve moral balance by slanting his vocabulary throughout to stress Ahab's malevolence (not least by giving him his loaded name), and by making Ishmael the vehicle of the story, he has invested much emotion and rhetoric on Ahab's side; as Stanley Geist puts it, "that grief and greatness were inseparable was Melville's ripest conviction." In Ahab he expresses something of what he praised in Hawthorne, the type he himself repeated in Pierre, Ethan Allen, and Moredock, the man who "declares himself a sovereign nature (in himself) amid the powers of heaven, hell, and earth."[63] Pierre likewise, a moral extremist defying the normal codes, and "ringed . . . in with the grief of Eternity," enables Melville to express something obsessionally powerful, something expressed in self-purgation. It is this purgation aspect which is ultimately the unsatisfactory thing about Ahab and Pierre. Melville knows of attitudes better than those he projects in these hero-victims, and the novels prove it. But the "unmanageable" element indulges itself, heightening the book's grandeur but its fulsomeness likewise. "We are not convinced that [Melville] is not inflating his theme, is not giving it a bulk it cannot properly bear," Dr Tillyard observes in *The Epic Strain in the English Novel*, and one would agree.

Ahab's species, of course, is that of heroic rebel. His presentation,[64] preluded by Ishmael's "foreboding shivers" (Melville is too little content to let his material make its own effect), is of the massive, scarred figure with the grandeur and woe of the Miltonic Satan, the Radcliffian Schedoni, the Shelleyan Prometheus, the Byronic Lara (*Lara*, I. xvii–xix, is particularly relevant), and the "Daemonic persons" Goethe describes in *Truth and Poetry*:

> a tremendous energy seems to be seated in them, and they exercise a wonderful power over all creatures and even over the elements; and, indeed, who shall say how much further such influence may extend? All the moral powers combined are of no avail against them . . . and they are to be overcome by nothing but the universe itself . . . *Nemo contra Deum nisi Deus ipse*.[65]

The recurrence of this Latin tag in *Pierre*,[66] and the

Enceladus story there,[67] suggest a direct Goethean influence, for Goethe also writes of "the Titanic, gigantic, heaven-storming character":

Tantalus, Ixion, Sisyphus, were also my saints. Admitted to the society of the gods, they would not deport themselves submissively enough, but by their haughty bearing as guests, provoked the anger of their host and patron, and drew upon themselves a sorrowful banishment.[68]

Ahab may owe something also to the hero of Fenimore Cooper's *Red Rover*. Melville reviewed a re-issue of this in 1850 and commented, "Long ago, and far inland, we read it in our uncritical days, and enjoyed it as much as thousands of the rising generation will when supplied with such an entertaining volume." It resembles *Moby Dick* in, for instance, the *Royal Caroline*'s sinking, the turbulent crew chosen from many nations, Roderick the timid lad devoted to his master, and most of all the Rover himself, despotically commanding, "settled and austere," a "reckless, wayward being," with "thoughtful and clouded brow . . . brooding reveries." The Rover lives up to the description the introduction gives of him:

a nature quick in intellect, endowed with great force of will, possessing every advantage of social position and culture in early life, but wildly passionate and wayward, [and having] violently thrown off all social restraint and cast itself loose on the stormy side of life; an outlaw in spirit.

(Incidentally, the sea-fight in *The Red Rover* brings strongly to mind that in *Israel Potter*, and may well have affected Melville's narrative.) Ahab is vastly more striking than the Rover; his place is with what Mario Praz calls "the Fatal Men of the Romantics." Yet Melville greatly admired Cooper, and it would be strange if *Moby Dick* owed nothing to the most famous previous American mystery novel of sea-adventure.

"One of Shakespeare's modes of creating characters," Coleridge observes, "is to conceive any one intellectual or moral faculty in morbid excess." Melville was reading Coleridge as well as Shakespeare, and it may be, Leon Howard suggests, that he echoes this in his comment that Ahab has "a half wilful morbidness at the bottom of his nature" and that "all men tragically great are made so through a certain morbidness . . . all mortal greatness is but disease."[69] Ahab's moral unfolding must now be examined, to see how far his greatness is disease.

At first still linked to society, with a new-married wife and soon a son, "Ahab has his humanities." At first Ishmael feels sympathy and sorrow for him, as well as curiosity. Peleg bears witness to his resourceful seamanship when the *Pequod* was dismasted off Japan—"Life was what Captain Ahab and I was thinking of; and how to save all hands." From "a considerating touch of humanity" Ahab refrains from stumping the quarter-deck by night, and he smokes a pipe, "meant for sereneness," until in an unsociable impulse he flings it overboard. (Melville's own appreciation of the creature comforts occurs amply in his novels and letters, and in the comments of his friends.) But steadily the obsessive mania asserts itself. The objects of his defiance are twin aspects of supernatural power—the lightning which scarred him, the whale which maimed him. Fedallah, smuggled aboard with his fellows to be Ahab's director in the hunt for the whale, his auxiliary in defying God's fire, is his evil spirit, and Ahab's boat-crew when Moby Dick is attacked are secret and in effect diabolical aliens. Fedallah, "perched aloft . . . his turban and the moon companions in one sky," first sights the spout superstitiously taken to be Moby Dick's jet,[70] though Ahab himself, eighty-two chapters later, first actually sights the whale. Along with the try-works scene, that of "The Candles" is the one which most sensationally expresses Ahab's alienation from God and man, and addiction to Satanic pride. This stage of his development needs some attention.

The "Candles" scene is influenced by, and should be seen against, the supernatural fires of Hawthorne's "Young Goodman Brown." In this story, illuminated by "four blazing pines, their tops aflame, their stems untouched, like candles at an evening meeting," a diabolically-possessed assembly of New England townsfolk joins in a witches' sabbath:

> As the red light arose and fell, a numerous congregation alternately shone forth, then disappeared in shadow, and again grew, as it were, out of the darkness. . . . [They sang] words which expressed all that our nature can conceive of sin, and darkly hinted at far more. . . . The four blazing pines threw up a loftier flame, and obscurely discovered shapes and visages of horror on the smoke wreaths above the impious assembly.

Though Hawthorne's four pines become Melville's three masts, Melville's derivation is evident. But whereas Hawthorne's effects are single, his assembly diabolic, his candles infernal, Melville's, as his other symbols, are complex, offering a differing interpretation to each nature. To Ishmael, the St Elmo's fire is "God's burning finger" laid on the ship, to Stubb, "a sign of good luck," to Starbuck, God's warning. But Ahab takes it to symbolise supreme tyranny, and he stands against it:

> "Hand me those mainmast links there; I would fain feel this pulse; and let mine beat against it; blood against fire! So." Then turning, the last link held fast in his left hand, he put his foot upon the Parsee; and with fixed upward eye, and high-flung right arm, he stood erect before the lofty tri-pointed flames.[71]

God is, in effect, warning against sin; along with Ishmael, Starbuck is the most reliable focus of judgment in the book. But Ahab makes this scene one of the peaks of his defiance, his confrontation of supreme power in one of its two great aspects. Immediately before, he has destroyed the quadrant by which he observed the sun; immediately after, he outrages the codes of seamanship,[72] the compasses are found to be reversed by the electric storm, and the log-line breaks.[73] The corposant flames flashing upwards from the mastheads are linked to the other symbol of "speechless, placeless power"—"the white flame but lights the way to the White Whale."[74] Challenging the symbolic fire and the symbolic creature (whether these be agents or principals) Ahab puts himself outside (above, he would say) nature and mankind. "Though nominally included in the census of Christendom, he was still an alien to it . . . in his inclement, howling old age, Ahab's soul, shut up in the caved trunk of his body, there fed upon the sullen paws of its gloom."[75] With "intense bigotry of purpose,"[76] "gaunt and ribbed, like the black sand beach after some strong tide has been gnawing it,"[77] Ahab, "the Fates' lieutenant," is his own law; "Ahab is for ever Ahab."[78] The measure of his repudiation of humanity is the "unconditional and utter rejection" of the *Rachel*'s appeal for help in an errand of paternal mercy (Captain Gardiner entreats him in terms of Christian doctrine and of family affection alike—"Do to me as you would have me do to you in the like case. For *you* too have a boy, Captain Ahab—though but a child, and nestling safely at home now").[79] Shortly afterwards Ahab confesses to Starbuck his "desolation of solitude," "whole oceans away from that young girl I wedded past fifty, and sailed for Cape Horn the next day, leaving but one dent in my marriage pillow—wife? wife?—rather a widow with her husband alive."[80] In the strongest contrast with Ahab's rejection of parenthood and with the destructiveness of his profession (man's version of "vulturism") is the chapter on the whale-mothers and their offspring, in its reverent treatment of natural procreativeness. Yet enough of intermittent humanity diversifies Ahab's monomania to make him genuinely a tragic figure, a great man in ruin.

In *The Eccentric Design* Marius Bewley deprecates "that romantic exaltation of Ahab which has resulted in missing Melville's point,"[81] and to trace the book's moral enquiry means looking at other points of reference. The first is Father Mapple's sermon. Mapple is drawn after "Father" Taylor, the Boston Methodist evangelist, whose sermon style, as reported in the *Knickerbocker Magazine* in 1849, was as suitable to his auditors as is Mapple's:

> The Bible, the Bible is the compass of life. Keep it always at hand. Steadily, steadily fix your eye on it. Study your bearing by it. Make yourself acquainted with all its points. It will serve you in calm and in storm, in the brightness of noonday, and amid the blackness of night: it will carry you over every sea, in every clime, and navigate you at last into the harbor of eternal rest.[82]

Such a man, if taken seriously (as Mapple is), will provide a strong standpoint. Mapple's prow-shaped pulpit itself occasions a significant comment:

> the Holy Bible rested on a projecting piece of scroll work, fashioned after a ship's fiddle-headed beak. What could be more full of meaning?—for the pulpit is ever this earth's foremost part; all the rest comes in the rear; the pulpit leads the world . . . Yes, the world's a ship on its passage out, and not a voyage complete; and the pulpit is its prow.[83]

After Mapple's prayer, "so deeply devout that he seemed kneeling and praying at the bottom of the sea," the congregation sings a hymn which drowns the sound of the storm, celebrating Jonah's deliverance from despair and from the prospect of death and hell:

> In black distress, I called my God,
>   When I could scarce believe him mine,
> He bowed his ear to my complaints—
>   No more the whale did me confine.

With speed he flew to my relief,
  As on a radiant dolphin borne;
The face of my Deliverer God
  Awful, yet bright, as lightning shone.

(The accepted text has these last two lines in reverse
order but the rhyme suggests it is wrong, and I have
ventured to change it.) Then Mapple preaches on
Jonah's disobedience and repentance. "If we obey God,
we must disobey ourselves, and it is in this disobeying
ourselves, wherein the hardness of obeying God consists."[84]
As heroic and self-dedicated as Ahab, he nevertheless
stands in fundamental contrast:

> Delight,—top-gallant delight is to him, who acknow-
> ledges no law or lord, but the Lord his God, and is
> only a patriot to Heaven. Delight is to him, whom all
> the waves of the billows of the seas of the boisterous
> mob can never shake from this sure Keel of the Ages.
> And eternal delight and deliciousness will be his, who,
> coming to lay him down, can say with his final breath
> —O Father!—chiefly known to me by Thy rod—
> mortal or immortal, here I die. I have striven to be
> Thine, more than to be this world's, or mine own.[85]

Mapple and Ahab both live under the magnetism of a
supreme Power, but their attitudes toward it are antithetical. The one's mission produces a noble confidence,
the other's, like Pierre's also, anguish and ravage not only
to the agent but to others as well. Yet assuming that
these attitudes are all, why side with Mapple rather than
with Ahab? Trust is no doubt more agreeable than
anguish, and Ahab's course and style are certainly not
recommended by his hysteria. But may this course and
style not be what is appropriate to the situation of man?
This now needs considering.

  In effect, Melville offers three kinds of relationship
which may hold mutually among the creatures of this
world, human and other, and three which may hold,

again mutually, between man and God. On the level of creatures there is love (or trust); hate (or malice); and, in between, acceptance (or resignation), not merely loving or hating but admitting the course of things, including accident, suffering, and struggle. These relationships are exhibited in *Moby Dick* respectively by, for instance, the whale-nursery; the "devilishness" that Ishmael attributes to the sharks or the "malice" that Ahab attributes to the White Whale; and the necessary "cannibalism" of creatures preying on each other to live. On the human level, there are social affections, with delight in the natural world; imperious and defiant will; and, in between, the normal struggle to live. And on the level of man and God there are faith and God's justice; hatred and God's malice; and, in between (to ignore mere credulity or heedlessness), agnosticism from man, inscrutability from God.

This is not to say that each item in each of these three triads corresponds to the equivalent one in the other two triads. It is partly to suggest something of the range of readings which makes *Moby Dick* peculiarly rich in effect, and partly to see where the participants in the story stand. Ahab, driven by hatred, imperious in self-will, "deliriously" transferring to the White Whale his sense of "malicious agencies," transcends the order of things and sins in anger and pride. "His sin, in the minor sense," Yvor Winters observes, "is monomaniac vengeance; in the major, the will to destroy the spirit of evil itself, an intention blasphemous because beyond human powers and infringing upon the purposes of God."[86] The White Whale need not, in fact, be read as the spirit of evil; "each man reads his own peculiar lesson according to his own peculiar mind and mood." But Ahab reads him so.

Mapple's position is that of faith and devotion, obedience to the Old Testament God, submission to His will, humility which does not invade His province. These

evident landmarks from which bearings are taken on
Ahab's erroneous course cannot but help guide our judgment. Yet if Calvinistic faith had sufficed to Melville's
forebears it did not suffice to him. Ahab exceeds in
defiance, but Mapple exceeds in conviction. Melville
embodies in Mapple his own powerful sense of the Cal-
vinist tradition but he cannot endorse this tradition save
in respect of its ardour. He embodies in Ahab an antithetical position and an equal ardour, and is emotionally seized by him, as he is by Mapple too. But in the
White Whale he embodies his own agnostic sense that
supreme Power, if there be any, is ambiguous and
inscrutable. By its whiteness the whale symbolises ambiguity (as "The Whiteness of the Whale" explains). By
its featurelessness when viewed face to face (if it has a
face?) the whale's head symbolises inscrutability:

> In the great sperm whale, this high and mighty god-
> like dignity inherent in the brow is so immensely
> amplified, that gazing on it, in that full front view, you
> feel the Deity and the dread powers more forcibly than
> in beholding any other object in living nature. For you
> see no one point precisely; not one distinct feature is
> revealed; no nose, eyes, ears, or mouth; no face; he
> has none, proper; nothing but that one broad firma-
> ment of a forehead, plaited with riddles.[87]

"This aspect is sublime," Ishmael declares, and the
whale's most sublime characteristic is his silence. He has
no voice. A dissertation on Silence in *Pierre*,[88] comparable
with that on Whiteness in *Moby Dick*, was to deal again
with divine inscrutability; borrowing a phrase from
Emerson (who called character "a reserved force"), it
was to declare that Silence "speaks of the Reserved
Forces of Fate. Silence is the only Voice of our God."
The metaphysical signposts, then, point finally not
towards Mapple's trust or Ahab's hate but towards un-
certainty, ambiguousness. The moral signposts, however,

point finally towards charity, and this will be examined when Ishmael is considered.

As for Moby Dick himself, it is worth remembering that Melville might have been prompted by *The Red Rover* into a title like *The Black Captain*, but the book was "The Whale" in composition and *The Whale* or *Moby Dick* when published. For of course the subject is whales in general and this whale in particular. New England was rich in whaling stories. Emerson notes in his journal, on 19 February 1834, that a seaman told him of Old Tom, a white sperm whale which crushed whale-boats in its jaws. The *Knickerbocker Magazine* in May 1839 published "Mocha Dick, Or the White Whale of the Pacific," by an ex-naval officer Jeremiah Reynolds. This stresses the whale's size and whiteness ("He was as white as wool!"), tells how ships hailed each other with "Any news from Mocha Dick?" and how sailors took him "rather as a ferocious fiend of the deep, than a regular-built legitimate whale," gives a vigorous account of the killing, and praises American sailors and their enterprise.[89] This account, in an enthusiastic context of patriotic zeal, must have influenced Melville's own. From Joseph Hart's *Miriam Coffin, or, The Whale-Fisherman* (1834) comes one of *Moby Dick*'s preliminary extracts, as does the name Starbuck (mate of the *Grampus* in Hart's story), the Gayhead squaw prophesying doom,[90] and possibly Peleg, since one Peleg Folger owned the *Grampus*. Hart relates very vividly how the vessel was sunk by an enraged whale. But the most famous such incident, the chief and recognised source of the *Pequod*'s fate, is Owen Chase's *Narrative of the Most Extraordinary and Distressing Shipwreck of the Whale-Ship Essex* (1821). Melville's copy of this exists and records how while on the *Acushnet* he was lent the work by Chase's son. J. Ross Browne's *Etchings of a Whaling Cruise* (1846), which he had reviewed, also gave or at least recalled much to him. Browne's accounts of harpoonings and the chase would not discredit

F

Melville himself. His frontispiece, showing a whaler stripping blubber from a carcass, with sharks all round and the try-works belching smoke, recalls "The Cutting-In" in *Moby Dick*, and much more fully so does the description of the operation, which is strikingly similar to Melville's account. In *Moby Dick* the oblivion which overtakes mastheadmen in tropical seas,[91] the baling of the "case" or upper part of the whale's head,[92] the whale all but ramming the ship,[93] the cutting of "Bible leaves,"[94] the sailor asleep in the try-pot,[95] the whaling implements and processes, the mates' exhortations in the chase, the whale dying with its head to the sun—these and other details are close enough to Browne to suggest that Melville had the *Etchings* open for frequent reference. His "try-works" description virtually rewrites Browne,[96] though the latter half of the chapter with its moral-metaphysical commentary is entirely his own. His account of Nantucket he derives from Obed Macy's *History of Nantucket* (1835). The cetology comes from many sources, but in particular from William Scoresby's *Account of the Arctic Regions and Northern Whale Fishery* (1820), Thomas Beale's *Natural History of the Sperm Whale* (1839), and F. D. Bennett's *Narrative of a Whaling Voyage* (1846). Whales in general, "leviathanic revelations and allusions of all sorts," occasion an immense survey of Creation: round the whaling theme is organised an encyclopedia of its history and ramifications, and New England's great industry in its climactic phase gains an incomparable memorial. In all its modifications the whale had for Melville the fascination exerted on Sir Thomas Browne by the quincunx, with the added potency of its being the most magnificent of living creatures.

But Moby Dick is more than an economico-zoological phenomenon; he is a great whale and a great touchstone of conceptions. The most important point of his interpretation has been touched on already, that he is not, objectively considered, motiveless malignity or the spirit of evil; he is to each man according to each man's nature, and defining him is attempting, in Melville's phrase, "the classification of the constituents of a chaos."[97] As the doubloon[98] means to Ahab egotistical pride and stormy fate, to Starbuck faith and its troubling fluctuations, to Stubb the comic buffets of life, to Flask the value of nine hundred and sixty cigars, to the Manxman destruction, to Queequeg an old button, to Fedallah fire-worship, to Pip drowning, so Moby Dick is one thing to Flask ("very pugnacious about whales" but quite irreverent), another to Stubb ("A joker is the whale A-flourishing his tail"), another to Starbuck ("Vengeance on a dumb brute" is "worse than devil's madness"), another to Captain Boomer of the *Enderby*, and so on. Two things are important. One is that references to "infernal forethought of ferocity" and so forth arise from sailors' superstitions or Ahab's frame of mind. Exceptions to this generalisation, if any, are presumably due to oversight (or indeed to printing error).[99] The "malignant" version of the White Whale results from simplemindedness or mania, conveyed through the streams of consciousness and the interior monologues, which need to be read dramatically and not objectively. The other thing is that the nearest one gets to a guaranteed interpretation of what the whale symbolises is, as has just been suggested, an assertion of cosmic inscrutability which gives no answers but presents in turn the aspects of supreme beauty (Moby Dick's first appearance is serenely lovely),[100] supreme power (the breaching, for instance),[101] supreme dangerousness, and supreme invulnerability. Since Nature evinces "demonism" as well as goodness, and destructiveness as well as procreation, Deity in its inscrutability doubtless includes these too, supremely. But the anthropomorphism which would be implied in supreme malignity does not seem to be Melville's intention. A similar situation is found in Hardy's novels, which often seem to give the reader to understand that Fate is malicious and the President of the Immortals a sadist, which Hardy declared he did not mean. "The Whiteness of the Whale" includes symbolical significances ranging all the way from the colour of heavenly faith to the "colourless all-colour of atheism,"[102] and whiteness, by mixtures of its ingredients, provides all Nature's colourings. But Ahab's belief in supernatural malice can arise only from exasperation, mistaking the evidence and claiming more attention from inscrutability than man's relative smallness warrants. Exasperation is a form of pride. So, on a front far broader than Hawthorne's, Melville looks for the whole meaning, and in the whale and the hunt for it "goes beyond the moral to the metaphysical," as Vega Curl observes, and "strives to put all experience together."[103]

Yet the moral conclusion deserves attention not less than the metaphysical. Having looked at Mapple's theocentricity and Ahab's blasphemy, it remains to assess a few other moral attitudes, not least as further counterbalances to the "romantic exaltation of Ahab." One is found in Starbuck, the excellent officer, "uncommonly conscientious," "endued with a deep natural reverence," mellowed by his beloved young wife and child from the "original ruggedness of his nature" (as Ahab is not), the loyal but sane man who finds Ahab's obsession an affront to sense and nature. His destruction comes through his lack not of courage, of which he has plenty, but of independence. In that, of course, he is only being true to his professionalism; resistance to Ahab would be mutiny. Outraged by Ahab's recklessness, lacerated in his home affections by Ahab's destructiveness, tempted to murder him, knowing (in an echo of Mapple) that "I disobey my God in obeying him,"[104] he is overcome by his instincts of obedience. Starbuck is there as human decency, and though destroyed by his subservience he has said enough to show Ahab's violence for what it is.

Another striking contrast to Ahab is Captain Boomer of the *Samuel Enderby*. Of this vessel, and "the famous whaling-house of Enderby & Sons," Melville gives an account substantial enough to establish that Boomer represents the central vigour of the profession and stands for a responsible attitude. "A darkly-tanned, burly, good-natured, fine-looking man, of sixty or thereabouts," like Ahab he is also mutilated by Moby Dick, but unlike Ahab he is cheerfully philosophical, appreciates the "noble great whale," is grateful for his survival, jokes about his whale-bone arm, and determines to leave well alone. To suffer as Ahab has suffered without being affected as Ahab is affected is clearly possible—but possible for a Boomer, not for an Ahab, for whom the compulsion is absolute, and who, to Boomer's nonchalance about Moby Dick, exclaims, "He's all a magnet!" Boomer's view is right in terms of cheerfulness and good sense. But these are limited qualities only, and the limitation is, no doubt, jocularly though not disapprovingly reflected in his name. Into him Melville put his own jocular-resilient strain, as into Ahab he put the compulsive extravagance which drove him through *Mardi* or *Pierre* and the rigour of purpose which, as Hawthorne recorded of his visit in Liverpool, kept him "wandering to-and-fro over these deserts [of speculation and unorthodoxy], as dismal and monotonous as these sandhills amid which we were sitting." Hawthorne goes on:

He can neither believe, nor be comfortable in his unbelief, and he is too honest and courageous not to try to do one or the other. If he were a religious man, he would be one of the most truly religious and reverential; he has a very high and noble nature, and better worth immortality than most of us.[105]

Ahab is likewise better worth immortality than Boomer.

It is Ishmael, however, who conveys the total book all together, and best counterpoises the "romantic exaltation of Ahab." He is there not to provide a single clear focus—such a thing would go against the book's ambivalences and inclusiveness. In one sense he is not much there at all; as Walter Bezanson observes in "Moby-Dick: Work of Art," "forecastle Ishmael drops in and out of the narrative with such abandon that at times the reader wonders if he has fallen overboard."[106] But in another sense, as Mr Bezanson points out, "the Ishmael voice is there every moment from the genesis of the fiction in 'Call me Ishmael' to the final revelation of the Epilogue." He provides tones of feeling to relieve Ahab's blackness. Even his initial misanthropy is comically given. He indulges in irreverent incongruities, jokes of all kinds, including ribald and indeed phallic ones ("The Cassock"), and the tall-story folk-humour in which Melville abounds. "Beneath Ishmael's mask of hypochondria," to quote Mr Bezanson again, "is the healthy grimace of a man who stands braced to receive 'the universal thump'." One notes the resilience with which, having scrutinised the whalemen's memorials in the chapel, he "grew merry again"—"and therefore three cheers for Nantucket, and come a stove boat and stove body when they will, for stave my soul, Jove himself cannot."[107] He has a passion for ideas, old lore, far places, "the overwhelming idea of the great whale." He is learned, but he is excited by action and practical processes to which he gives, Mr Bezanson well remarks, "ceremonial dignity." But in addition he is the one person seen capable of spiritual rebirth and survival. Ahab, it is true, is reborn by the effect of his mutilations, but towards darkness and death; the book relates that change as being in effect completed. The other characters are set fast in their natures. But Ishmael is redeemed from his "splintered heart and maddened hand" by Queequeg's goodness, and their union is symbolised later by the monkey-rope, that "elongated Siamese ligature" ensuring their joint safety or danger.[108] His prejudices are bent by love;[109] he is charitable to all faiths.[110] Squeezing the sperm-oil he feels "divinely free from all ill-will, or petulance, or malice, of any sort whatever" and

> perceive[s] that in all cases man must eventually lower, or at least shift, his conceit of attainable felicity; not placing it anywhere in the intellect or fancy; but in the wife, the heart, the bed, the table, the saddle, the fireside, the country.[111]

From a "wild, mystical, sympathetical feeling" he swears Ahab's oath, but in the try-works chapter he sees the ship as a "red hell" and feels "a stark, bewildered feeling as of death." Recovering, he achieves that sense of inter-related darkness and light with which the chapter ends. The latest glimpse of him is long after the *Pequod*'s sinking, in that "fine gam" with the *Samuel Enderby* so cheerfully recorded.[112] By calling him Ishmael, Melville certainly implied, initially, the "wild man; his hand . . . against every man" of Genesis, xvi. 12; but he knew that the rest of the Bible's account is in terms of God's favour. Re-deemed to charity by primitive brotherliness, his soul superior to fate's buffets,[113] his "fog" of doubts enkindled with "divine intuitions . . . neither believer nor infidel,"[114] and finding in the nursing whales an analogy to the "eternal mildness of joy" amidst his own "tornadoed Atlantic," Ishmael, the book's consciousness, is the true criterion of Ahab's monomania, and what Melville wants to say about human nature. While both moralities, of revenge and acceptance, are essential to the complex of the book's feelings, and are indeed explicitly interwoven in "The Symphony" (that significantly-named chapter in the key-position immediately before the climax-disaster), the morality which, after all the heroic defiance, is beauti-fully designed to prevail is the latter, that of the Epilogue. Here, on a "soft and dirge-like main," accompanied by unharming sharks and inoffensive sea-hawks, "buoyed up" by the coffin of the kindly Queequeg, and rescued by the *Rachel* whose pitiful search for her missing men Ahab had refused to join, Ishmael, whose name as we may recall and as the Bible-reading Melville would know means "God shall hear," delivers the last words of reticent serenity.

REFERENCES

1. *Letters*, p. 130.
2. *Letters*, p. 128.
3. *P.*, BK. XXI, sect. i.
4. *P.*, BK. XXV, sect. iii.
5. *Letters*, p. 124.
6. *M.*, ch. clxxx (st. ed., II. 324).
7. "Hawthorne and his Mosses," in *The Shock of Recognition*, ed. Edmund Wilson, 1956, pp. 192–4; originally in the *Literary World*, Aug. 17, 24, 1850.
8. *M.D.*, ch. xcv (st. ed., ch. xcvi; II. 177).
9. *M.D.*, *loc. cit.* (st. ed., II. 181).
10. "The Encantadas," Sketch Second.
11. *Letters*, p. 133.
12. *M.D.*, ch. cxii (st. ed., ch. cxiii; II. 261).
13. R. W. Emerson, *Essays: First Series*, "Over-Soul."
14. R. W. Emerson, *Essays: Second Series*, "Nature."
15. *P.*, BK. XXV, sect. iv.
16. *Letters*, p. 138.
17. *Letters*, p. 142.
18. Metcalf, p. 133.
19. *Letters*, p. 109.
20. Perry Miller, *The Raven and the Whale*, 1956, p. 29.
21. *M.D.*, ch. xlvii (st. ed., xlviii; I. 273).
22. *M.D.*, ch. xlvi (st. ed., ch. xlvii).
23. *M.D.*, ch. xcv (st. ed., ch. xcvi).
24. *M.D.*, ch. cxviii (st. ed., ch. cxix).
25. *M.D.*, ch. xlvii (st. ed., ch. xlviii).
26. *M.D.*, ch. lviii (st. ed., ch. lix).
27. *M.D.*, chs. lx, lxxx (st. ed., chs. lxi, lxxxi).
28. *M.D.*, ch. lxxxvi (st. ed., ch. lxxxvii).
29. *M.D.*, ch. l (st. ed., ch. li; I. 293).
30. *M.D.*, ch. cxxxii (st. ed., ch. cxxxiii; II. 333).
31. *M.D.*, ch. lx (st. ed., ch. lxi; II. 2–3).
32. *M.D.*, ch. cxxxiv (st. ed., ch. cxxxv; II. 366).
33. *M.D.*, ch. lxxxvi (st. ed., ch. lxxxvii; II. 132–5).
34. *Sartor Resartus*, I. iv.
35. *Sartor Resartus*, I. v.
36. *Sartor Resartus*, I. x.
37. *Sartor Resartus*, III. iii.
38. *Sartor Resartus*, I. x, xi.
39. *M.D.*, ch. xxxv (st. ed., ch. xxxvi; I. 204).
40. *Letters*, p. 79.
41. *Sartor Resartus*, I. ii.

42. R. W. Emerson, *Essays: First Series*, "Compensation."

43. *Letters*, p. 142.

44. Yvor Winters, "Herman Melville and the Problems of Moral Navigation," in *In Defense of Reason*, 1947, p. 221.

45. *M.D.*, ch. lxix (st. ed., ch. lxx; ii. 38).

46. *M.D.*, ch. xxxi (st. ed., ch. xxxii; i. 176).

47. *M.D.*, ch. xxxiv (st. ed., ch. xxxv; i. 198).

48. *M.D.*, ch. xl (st. ed., ch. xli; i. 229).

49. *M.D.*, ch. xci (st. ed., ch. xcii; ii. 162).

50. *M.D.*, ch. cxxxiv (st. ed., ch. cxxxv; ii. 367).

51. *M.D.*, ed. Willard Thorp, 1947, p. xvii.

52. *Letters*, p. 146.

53. Stanley Geist, *Herman Melville; The Tragic Vision and the Heroic Ideal*, 1939, p. 44.

54. R. W. Emerson, *Essays: First Series*, "Spiritual Laws."

55. *M.D.*, ch. cxxxi (st. ed., ch. cxxxii; ii. 329).

56. *M.D.*, ch. xxiii (st. ed., i. 132–3).

57. *M.D.*, ch. lvii (st. ed., ch. lviii; i. 348–9).

58. Richard Chase, *Herman Melville*, 1949, p. 78.

59. *M.D.*, ch. xxxii (st. ed., ch. xxxiii; i. 181).

60. *M.D.*, ch. xxvi (st. ed., ch. xxvii; i. 149).

61. *M.D.*, ch. xxvii (st. ed., ch. xxviii; i. 152–4).

62. *M.D.*, ch. cxxxiv (st. ed., ch. cxxxv; ii. 367).

63. *Letters*, p. 124.

64. *M.D.*, ch. xxvii (st. ed., ch. xxviii; i. 152–5).

65. *The Autobiography of Goethe: Truth and Poetry from my own Life*, tr. J. Oxenford, 2 vols., 1848–9, ii. 159. In this edition Melville read *Dichtung und Wahrheit*.

66. *P.*, bk. i, sect. iv.

67. *P.*, bk. xxv, sects. iv–v.

68. Goethe, *Autobiography*, ii. 39.

69. *M.D.*, ch. xvi (st. ed., i. 92).

70. *M.D.*, ch. l (st. ed., ch. li; i. 293).

71. *M.D.*, ch. cxviii (st. ed., ch. cxix; ii. 281).

72. *M.D.*, chs. cxix–xx (st. ed., chs. cxx–xxi).

73. *M.D.*, chs. cxxiii–iv (st. ed., chs. cxxiv–v).

74. *M.D.*, ch. cxviii (st. ed., ch. cxix; ii. 281).

75. *M.D.*, ch. xxxiii (st. ed., ch. xxxiv; i. 190).

76. *M.D.*, ch. xxxv (st. ed., ch. xxxvi; i. 200).

77. *M.D.*, ch. lxxxvi (st. ed., ch. lxxxvii; ii. 129).

78. *M.D.*, ch. cxxxiii (st. ed., ch. cxxxiv; ii. 352).

79. *M.D.*, ch. cxxxvii (st. ed., ch. cxxxviii; ii. 314).

80. *M.D.*, ch. cxxxi (st. ed., ch. cxxxii; ii. 328).

81. Marius Bewley, *The Eccentric Design*, p. 193.

82. Quoted by Perry Miller, *The Raven and the Whale*, p. 20.

83. *M.D.*, ch. viii (st. ed., i. 48).

84. *M.D.*, ch. ix (st. ed., i. 51).

85. *M.D.*, ch. ix (st. ed., i. 59).

86. Yvor Winters, *In Defense of Reason*, p. 211.

87. *M.D.*, ch. lxxviii (st. ed., ch. lxxix; ii. 82–3).

88. *P.*, BK. XIV, sects. i–ii.
89. Perry Miller, *The Raven and the Whale*, p. 21.
90. *M.D.*, ch. xvi (st. ed., I. 100).
91. *M.D.*, ch. xxxiv (st. ed., ch. xxxv).
92. *M.D.*, chs. lxxvi–vii (st. ed., chs. lxxvii–viii).
93. *M.D.*, ch. lxxii (st. ed., ch. lxxiii).
94. *M.D.*, ch. xciv (st. ed., ch. xcv).
95. *M.D.*, ch. xcv (st. ed., ch. xcvi).
96. Cf. J. Ross Browne, *Etchings of a Whaling Cruise*, 1846, pp. 60–64.
97. *M.D.*, ch. xxxi (st. ed., ch. xxxii; I. 164).
98. *M.D.*, ch. xcviii (st. ed., ch. xcix).
99. Some editions read "seeing malice" in ch. xl where the Standard Edition reads, presumably rightly, "seeming malice" (st. ed., ch. xli; I. 229). Melville's texts are often blemished by misprints.
100. *M.D.*, ch. cxxxii (st. ed., ch. cxxxiii; II. 333–5).
101. *M.D.*, ch. cxxxiii (st. ed., ch. cxxxiv; II. 346–7).
102. *M.D.*, ch. xli (st. ed., ch. xlii; I. 243).
103. Vega Curl, *Pasteboard Masks*, 1931, p. 14.
104. *M.D.*, ch. cxxxiv (st. ed., ch. cxxxv; II. 356).
105. Metcalf, p. 161.
106. Walter E. Bezanson, "Moby-Dick: Work of Art," in *Moby-Dick: Centennial Essays*, edd. Tyrus Hillway and Luther S. Mansfield, 1953, p. 41.
107. *M.D.*, ch. vii (st. ed., I. 45).
108. *M.D.*, ch. lxxi (st. ed., ch. lxxii; II. 48).
109. *M.D.*, ch. xi (st. ed., I. 66).
110. *M.D.*, ch. xvii (st. ed., I. 102).
111. *M.D.*, ch. xciii (st. ed., ch. xciv; II. 172).
112. *M.D.*, ch. c (st. ed., ch. ci; II. 206).
113. *M.D.*, ch. xlviii (st. ed., ch. xlix; I. 286).
114. *M.D.*, ch. lxxxiv (st. ed., ch. lxxxv; II. 117).

CHAPTER VI

PIERRE: OR, THE AMBIGUITIES

When Margaret Fuller announced, "I accept the universe," Carlyle made the famous comment, "Gad! she'd better!" Ahab is one who cannot accept it, Pierre one who thinks to accept it (the universe, that is, as contrasted with society), and finds he has taken on something tragically beyond him. "I even fancied to myself," Goethe says self-mockingly in his autobiography, "that [God] might even be in arrears to me, and I was daring enough to think that I had something to forgive Him."[1] By the end, Pierre might say as much, but in despair. The "rural bowl of milk" which Melville promised Sophia Hawthorne to follow *Moby Dick*[2] turned into a very strange draught.

Astonishing in range and richness, *Pierre* is ambiguous both in meaning and technique, but fruitfully ambiguous, in that it sets the curiosity actively to work. To Bentley Melville described it as a book "possessing unquestionable novelty, as regards my former ones,— treating of utterly new scenes and characters;—and, as I believe, very much more calculated for popularity than any thing you have yet published of mine."[3] Bentley declined it unless it received "absolutely necessary" alterations, and doubtless felt himself vindicated when, published elsewhere without these, it sold miserably. Extravagant, it nevertheless has great power, and it gives an intense impression that this had to be said. "We that write and print have all our books predestinated," Melville had told Evert Duyckinck.[4] That he should have expected popularity is strange, for he had expressed to

Lemuel Shaw "my earnest desire to write those sort of books which are said to 'fail',"[5] and though James Hanley has called it, "after *Moby Dick*, the book to read,"[6] *Pierre* looks like an intended product of that earnest desire. Indeed, the hero, who courts earthly failure for a transcendental end, reflects as Ahab had done one side of Melville, though not the whole, and the stimulus of the book lies in the conflicting views it provokes as to this intransigence.

John Stuart Mill asserts that the modern poet must suffer since his temperament is at odds with contemporary society, at odds

> not from mortified vanity, but from the poetic temperament itself, under the arrangements of society made by and for harder natures; and in the world, which, for any but the insensitive, is not a place of contentment ever, nor of peace till after many a hard-fought battle.[7]

Pierre raises the problem of Melville's public, and its incomprehension of him. His biographers have used his increasing alienation as a stick to beat the Philistines with. "What a madness & anguish it is," Melville wrote to Evert Duyckinck when *Mardi* was under attack, "that an author can never—under no conceivable circumstances—be at all frank with his readers."[8] Duyckinck himself, while praising *Moby Dick* in the *Literary World*, deplored in it the "piratical running down of creeds and opinions . . . the most sacred associations of life violated and defaced."[9] To Bentley, in July 1851, Melville struck against the public taste:

> This country & nearly all its affairs are governed by sturdy backwoodsmen—noble fellows enough, but not at all literary, & who care not a fig for any authors except those who write those most saleable of all books nowadays—i e— the newspapers, & magazines.[10]

Supporting a family he needed success, yet success on easy terms would be treachery. He bought Goethe's autobiography, *Poetry and Truth*, in 1849 and marked in it such passages as

> In the end, man is always driven back upon himself, and it seems as if the Divinity had taken a position towards men so as not always to respond to their reverence, trust, and love, at least not in the precise moment of need. . . . The man who cannot enjoy his own natural gifts in silence, and find his reward in the exercise of them, but must wait for their recognition and appreciation by others, will generally find himself but badly off.[11]

This sense of isolated virtue is the basis of the tragedy in *Pierre*. Yet, sadly short though the public fell in its support, Melville had challenged its taste radically, and he would doubtless have felt himself to have failed had he found ready acceptance. That the book's reception was distressing is less surprising than the fact that against abuse (some of it very strong) there was considerable approval (some of it very intelligent). Even nowadays *Pierre* is difficult to come to terms with, and it is not strange that readers of the eighteen-fifties were not disposed to try very hard.

Ambiguity is the note of the subtitle and of the book's manner and matter; it is indeed what *Pierre* is about. The plot is the life story of an extreme idealist, and a presentation (though not an elucidation) of the bewilderment involved in moral choices, ambiguous values, uncertain evidence, and ambivalent motives. Autobiographical detail abounds, but this certainly does not warrant the assumption sometimes made (for instance by Raymond Weaver and Lewis Mumford)[12] that Melville's parents were like Pierre's, or that most items refer back from Pierre's situation to Melville's. The narrative framework is used to display moral and metaphysical questions ranging from the validity of religious institutions, through truth and illusion in domestic affections and personal motives, to the sanctions for moral conduct, the confusions of good and evil, the nature of reality, and the bases of personality. Lewis Mumford has made the point that "*Pierre* is one of the first novels in which the self is treated as anything but a unit whose parts consist of the same material, with the grain, as it were, running the same way."

Melville unites the extravagances of nineteenth-century melodrama with those of the Gothick novel and of Jacobean tragedy (Pierre's relationship with Isabel is uncertainly incestuous), with sentimental pastoralism, farce, metaphysical speculation, and the unconvincing supernatural. By turns the book is gay, sugary, bitter, despairing, sardonic, hysterical, brightly trivial, oracularly impressive. The styles are the oddest ever devised by a great writer. Carlylian twists of syntax, more-than-Carlylian neologisms, Biblical rhythms, harmonies from Browne, discourse flavoured with Emerson, rhapsodies that read like a parody of Shelley—these are only a few of the stylistic bedfellows. Sometimes one thinks of Lamb, sometimes of Hawthorne, sometimes of Disraeli or Bulwer-Lytton (*Pelham*, it may be recalled, was read on the *Neversink*). At times an analytical subtlety seems to prefigure Henry James. More often Melville outgoes the figurative excesses of Jacobean drama; "The fringed curtains of thine eye advance," in *The Tempest*, is the kind of thing weirdly outdone, for instance, in "The striped tigers of his chestnut eyes leaped in their lashed cages with a fierce delight." And what is one to say of "An infixing stillness now thrust a long rivet through the night, and fast nailed it to this side of the world"—what, except that flamboyance can make enjoyable even the absurd? Some of the dialogue is preposterous beyond belief. Yet, while most of *Pierre* is unlikely, and some of it exasperating, little of it is dull. It beguiles by its wealth of

invention, its range of styles, its vigour of idea—and, if for
nothing else, by the hope of finding more words like
"patriarchalness," "preambillically," "gladiatorianism,"
and "impassionedments."

In its moral exploration the book is concerned with
three main positions; conventional worldliness, "virtuous
expediency," and moral absolutism. The qualities of most
of the participants are clear enough—Mrs Glendinning, Pierre's mother, fashioned by Infinite Haughtiness,[13]
represents the most unflinching patrician worldliness; Mr Falsgrave is the ecclesiastic "entangled by all
fleshly alliances";[14] Charlie Millthorpe is the decent
trivial hack, Lucy the spirit of true love, a "strange
heavenly influence."[15] None is deeply realised, but their
positions are clear. Isabel, and Plotinus Plinlimmon the
expedient philosopher, are more puzzling. Isabel is as
elfin a character as fiction can offer. Haunting, mysterious, captivating (to Pierre, though hardly to the reader),
she suggests the romantic enchantress (La Belle Dame,
and so on), though not for an instant can Melville induce
any willing suspension of disbelief. Melville had *Hamlet*
in mind while writing, and his idealist hero to whom the
world had seemed fair is brought by this virtually supernatural visitant to realise a hidden sin, to purge which he
so overstrains himself as to destroy his moral nature.
Isabel, who in his idealising mood is the test of "his
highest and most glorious duty,"[16] has by his last speech
become ambiguously "wife or sister, saint or fiend,"[17]
and, as she dies over his dead body, "her long hair ran
over him, and arboured him in ebon vines."[18] Whether
she is the fatal temptation to attempt absolute virtue, or
the happiness-dispelling initiation into knowledge of sin,
she lures Pierre to a fate which Lucy, like Ophelia, cannot avert.

Plinlimmon is more interesting. Welsh by origin,
Tennesseean by birth, equable yet inscrutable, named
after a mystical philosopher, Grand Master of the nature-

crank Apostles who symbolically inhabit an abandoned church (being high-minded but not Christian), originator of the treatise on "Chronometricals and Horologicals," yet never known to work or read or write (the treatise being a disciple's report), preferring curaçao to philosophy, he "leers" down on Pierre from his high chamber (like Teufelsdröckh's "old calmness and fixity" in his "speculum or watch-tower"). In his "steady observant blue-eyed countenance" are combined features of the young Apollo and the aged Saturn, "a remarkable face of repose,—repose neither divine nor human, nor anything made up of either or both—but a repose separate and apart," giving observers "a notion of something not before included in their scheme of the universe."[19] These last words hint, perhaps unintentionally, at Melville's joke that Emerson, "had he lived in those days when the world was made . . . might have offered some valuable suggestions."[20] Plinlimmon, in any case, is satire on Emersonian traits. His Welshness may point at "Waldo"; the loftiness of Platonic philosophy (Plotinus) and the mountain (Plynlimon) presumably reflect Transcendentalism's Platonic-idealistic aspirations; and, together with Plinlimmon's high-minded aspect but easy-going conduct, the "virtuous expediency" of his treatise may relate to the Transcendental "I-accept-the-Universe" and to Emerson's unconcern for consistency. Many features reappear in *The Confidence-Man*'s Mark Winsome, another Emersonian avatar, with his "pellucid blue eye," youthful face and aged brow, passionlessness, Platonism, condescension, non-benevolence, and rejection of consistency. True, Plinlimmon drinks curaçao and is a Tennesseean; Winsome drinks iced water and is a Yankee ("this Plato who talks thro' his nose" is how Melville described Emerson);[21] and no-one could accuse Emerson of not reading or writing. But the doctrines of "Chronometricals and Horologicals" recur, in recognisably Emersonian fashion, when Mark Winsome explains in

The Confidence-Man how his philosophical principles and
his worldly practice chime:

> Any philosophy that, being in operation contradic-
> tory to the ways of the world, tends to produce a charac-
> ter at odds with it, such a philosophy must necessarily
> be but a cheat and a dream. . . . Man came into this
> world, not to sit down and muse, not to befog himself
> with vain subtleties, but to gird up his loins and to
> work. Mystery is in the morning, and mystery in the
> night, and the beauty of mystery is everywhere; but
> still the plain truth remains, that mouth and purse
> must be filled. If, hitherto, you have supposed me a
> visionary, be undeceived.[22]

Plinlimmon is aspects of Emerson satirised. But this does
not mean that his treatise is satirised. Pierre, like Ahab,
is heroically absolutist, but casts himself for doom; the
treatise is unheroically empirical, but genuinely represents the best the world can hope to do. It may owe something also to the preface to Bishop Butler's *Sermons upon
Human Nature*, which argues that if man does his best he
need not aspire to perfection; in a Bible he bought in
1850 Melville marked the phrase "Be not righteous over-
much" (Ecclesiastes, VII. 16). The treatise follows a section which describes the Sermon on the Mount as the
greatest miracle of all religions, but contrasts its sublime
promises with the "downright positive falsity" of the
world.[23] The Sermon and the treatise thus juxtaposed
represent, respectively, absolute and conditional morality,
and Pierre's resistance to the treatise is explained as that
which a man feels when anything "unintendedly, as it
were, yet very palpably illustrates to him the intrinsic
incorrectness and non-excellence of both the theory and
the practice of his life."[24] This plain statement of Pierre's
error seems correspondingly to vouch for Plinlimmon's
counsels of virtuous expediency. Yet as with Ahab, one
senses that Melville is divided, between a passionate desire

to endorse Pierre against the world, and a balanced
wisdom of reasonable conformity.

This ambivalence is represented, again as with Ahab,
on the one hand by a strong slant of vocabulary stressing
Pierre's extravagance, and on the other by deeply felt
support of him against time-servers. The former attitude
is evident in his early sentimentalism (the silly brother-
sister play-acting with his mother, the pigeon shot so as
not to mark its breast, the fraternising with the colts, and
so on), and in the *motif* of valiant *naïveté*. The latter attitude is evident in the conception of the "victim" of
"Philosophy, Ideal Virtue," corrupted by crucifying
himself on the impossible, opposing "the very nature of
things," dreaming of himself as Enceladus, the Titan
born equally of Earth and Heaven, assaulting the invin-
cible. It is evident also in the echo of *Moby Dick*'s
Bulkington ("Still he [Pierre] like a demi-god bore up.
His soul's ship foresaw the inevitable rocks,"[25] "Bear thee
[Bulkington] grimly, demi-god! Up from the spray of thy
ocean-perishing—straight up, leaps thy apotheosis").[26]
Yet Melville's sympathy with Pierre is kept within
limits; recognising heroism, he yet presents Pierre's moral
corruption in terms which recall Ahab's obsession, admitting his "infinite rage and malice,"[27] his "grief of
Eternity" amid the rejoicings of Christmas,[28] his rejection of friendly overtures,[29] the "utmost hate" which is
"jubilantly welcome" to him,[30] and his isolation "solitary
as at the Pole."[31]

But if Pierre's course is inappropriate, the question
arises, "Inappropriate to what?" Like *Moby Dick* the
book is about supreme inscrutability. It is also about the
agony of spiritual autonomy in the absence of reliable
faith. The Sermon on the Mount sufficed for Babbalanja
in Serenia, but it does not work for Pierre; nor does any
such dogma as had satisfied Mapple; nor is there a
Queequeg to redeem Pierre by goodness, for he rejects
Lucy. Pierre has to plot his course in a world without

landmarks; later in life Melville marked in James Thomson's *Essays and Phantasies* some words from Spinoza —"All final causes are nothing but fiction."[32] Good and ill are ambiguous. Receiving a mysterious letter, Pierre feels a good angel prompting him to read it, a bad one prompting him to destroy it. He reads it but is "fatally hurt," for it reveals the existence of Isabel. Yet not to read it would be to avoid truth, to live in a Swiftian "perpetual possession of being well-deceived." Launched towards discovery he is launched also towards bewilderment; with an exhilaration of being "divinely dedicated" he seeks a sign from the Memnon Stone if his trust in virtue is misplaced, but it gives no sign except for a bird's song. Deity will not commit itself—"Silence is the only Voice of our God."[33] Philosophers claim to interpret messages from Heaven, but "how can a man get a Voice out of Silence?"[34] Thoreau also had pointed out that Silence "cannot be done into English. For six thousand years men have translated her with what fidelity belongs to each, and still she is little better than a sealed book."[35] And Teufelsdröckh suspected "an absentee God, sitting idle, ever since the first Sabbath."[36] "Doth not Scripture intimate," Melville sardonically asks, "that He holdeth all of us in the hollow of His hand?—a Hollow, truly!"[37] If God is mysterious, so also is man, his nature divided between earth and heaven, so that Pierre, even in his "reckless, sky-assaulting mood," is "nevertheless on one side the grandson of the sky."

To have committed himself with such passion to such problems is Melville's achievement in *Pierre*, though to compare *Pierre* with *Middlemarch*, which likewise explores idealism and experience, is to sense sharply how its "unmanageable" verbal and conceptual extravagance falls short of a convincing accomplishment. *Pierre* has neither organic form and character nor imaginative reality, and one is perpetually compelled to translate the symbolisation down into less improbable terms before it makes sense. The result fails as a novel, fails perhaps as any definable literary form, but fails more richly, inclusively, inventively, and certainly recklessly, than many successes succeed. Perhaps, as Melville wrote in reviewing Hawthorne, "It is better to fail in originality than to succeed in imitation."

REFERENCES

1. Goethe, *Autobiography*, I. 291.
2. *Letters*, p. 146.
3. *Letters*, p. 150.
4. *Letters*, p. 96.
5. *Letters*, p. 92.
6. *M.D.*, intro. James Hanley (Macdonald's Illustrated Classics), n.d., p. xvii.
7. J. S. Mill, "Writings of Alfred de Vigny," in *Dissertations and Discussions*, 1867, III. 323.
8. *Letters*, p. 96.
9. Leyda, I. 437.
10. *Letters*, p. 134.
11. Goethe, *Autobiography*, II. 37, 52.
12. Raymond M. Weaver, *Herman Melville*, pp. 54–62, takes the portraits of Mr and Mrs Glendinning to be tolerably accurate portrayals of Mr and Mrs Melville; Lewis Mumford, *Herman Melville*, pp. 15–18, deduces from the evidence of *Pierre* that "both Melville's father and his mother were monsters" and that Herman was so starved of affection that in *Pierre* he gave his hero no brothers and sisters "so that Pierre may absorb all his mother's warmth for himself." Warmth, indeed!
13. *P.*, BK. V, sect. i.
14. *P.*, BK. VIII, sect. vii.
15. *P.*, BK. XXV, sect. iii.
16. *P.*, BK. IX, sect. i.
17. *P.*, BK. XXVI, sect. vi.
18. *P.*, BK. XXVI, sect. vii.
19. *P.*, BK. XXII, sect. iii.
20. *Letters*, p. 79.
21. *Letters*, p. 79.
22. *C.M.*, ch. xxxvii.
23. *P.*, BK. XIV, sect. ii.
24. *P.*, *loc. cit.*
25. *P.*, BK. XXV, sect. iii.
26. *M.D.*, ch. xxiii (st. ed., I. 133).
27. *P.*, BK. XXI, sect. ii.
28. *P.*, BK. XXII, sect. iv.
29. *P.*, *loc. cit.*
30. *P.*, BK. XXV, sect. ii.
31. *P.*, *loc. cit.*
32. W. Braswell, *Melville's Religious Thought*, 1943, pp. 62–3.
33. *P.*, BK. XIV, sect. i.
34. *P.*, BK. XIV, sect. ii.
35. Henry Thoreau, *A Week on the Concord and Merrimack Rivers*, 1849, "Friday," conclusion.
36. Carlyle, *Sartor Resartus*, II. vii.
37. *P.*, BK. VII, sect. viii.

CHAPTER VII

ISRAEL POTTER; THE TALES; THE JOURNAL, 1856–1857

When in April 1857 Fitz-James O'Brien lamented in *Putnam's* that Melville had "turned away, habitually, of late years at least, to look in upon his own imaginations, and to cultivate his speculative faculties in a strange loose way," one suspects that his attention had lapsed since *Pierre*, though he did in fact oddly praise "The Encantadas" for its "charm, and truth, and hazy golden atmosphere," and he knew most of the stories. Between *Pierre* and *The Confidence-Man* occur some of Melville's clearest and strongest works, *Israel Potter* (1855), the best of the *Piazza Tales* (1856), and others—"Bartleby," "Cock-a-Doodle-Doo," "The Encantadas," "Benito Cereno," and "I and my Chimney." Not that they are unsymbolic— "much of these stories' materiality seems a minutely painted and deceptive screen erected across what is *really* taking place behind it—in Melville's mind," Jay Leyda has commented in his valuable introduction to the *Complete Stories*.[1] Nor are they all notable. But the best are very good writing indeed, and Michael Sadleir was not far wrong in asserting that, supreme though *Moby Dick* is, Melville's genius is here "more perfectly and skilfully revealed," and that "The Encantadas" and "Benito Cereno" "hold in the small compass of their beauty the essence of their author's supreme artistry."

In 1852 Melville offered Hawthorne a subject, the "Agatha" story. This relates the patient endurance of one Agatha Robertson (Melville calls her Robinson) during the seventeen years' unexplained absence of her husband, and the subsequent discovery that he had married again.

Neither Melville nor Hawthorne used the story, but the correspondence about it most interestingly illuminates the ways in which Melville's mind gathered relevant imaginative details, and also his interest in "patience, & endurance, & resignedness."[2] These qualities are a running theme in several stories of this period.

Israel Potter is based, with amplifications from other sources, on its hero's *Life and Remarkable Adventures* (1824). It is an excellently clear and animated narrative, and coming to it from *Pierre* one is astonished at the direct unaffected manner. The seafaring is most ably handled, in particular in the engagement between the *Serapis* and the *Bon Homme Richard*. Fenimore Cooper's sea-fight in *The Red Rover* seems to have given Melville some hints, but the verve of style is his own, and this scene has such vitality that it has merely to be read to be felt. The episodes in London are in their sordid picturesqueness almost as intense as *Redburn*'s pictures of Liverpool.[3] The antithesis is powerful between these scenes and the spacious landscapes of Israel's native Green Mountains, but one is not invited to symbolise; the contrast between natural grandeur and industrial hideousness comes over realistically. Melville may still be recalling, in a degree, the similar contrast in the *Confessions of an English Opium-Eater* but he renders his effects not at all derivatively. The other good things are the historical portraits, especially those of Benjamin Franklin, John Paul Jones, and Ethan Allen. Franklin is the best of these characterisations, portrayed with a mixture of admiration and satiric parody which foreshadows the similar treatment of Emerson in *The Confidence-Man*. A very intelligent mind indeed is here at work, enjoying its operations to the full. The combination of qualities in the book—strength, alertness, vigour and intelligence—makes *Israel Potter* notably satisfactory, though it somehow remains rather remote, and comes home upon the imagination less than *Typee*, or *Redburn*, or *White Jacket*, or *Moby Dick*, or *Billy Budd*.

The best of the tales do come home upon the imagination. The Duyckincks' *Cyclopædia* took "Bartleby" to be
"a quaint and fanciful portrait," but it is far more than
that. Its virtue lies in its memorable subject and its
wonderful control. The rhapsodies of *Moby Dick* and
Pierre are wholly absent, though the theme of tempera-
mental withdrawal (Bartleby is the supreme *isolato*) is one
which only the year before *Pierre* had handled with signs
of hysteria. Comedy is present in the fully-flavoured
humour, but the presiding impression is of the simple
intensity of Bartleby's courteous, dignified, uncom-
municating withdrawal, which obtains a moral ascen-
dency over the reader as over the narrator. The story has
its rhythm of increasing disquiet, from the quotidian
comedy of the lawyer's office to the stark crudity of the
prison and the physical death which succeeds the psycho-
logical. Bartleby's loneliness and dignity are expressed
with a spare, unforced concentration; he remains inviolable with the untouchability of the psychotic,
movingly rendered in his unexpressed despair.

"Cock-a-Doodle-Doo," almost contemporaneous in
composition, shows how various Melville's successes can
be. Lewis Mumford has called it one of his weakest tales,[4]
and one is up against the vagaries of Melville criticism,
for Melville rarely exceeded the grip he shows here. The
ability to create an expectation and keep it on the alert
is as striking as in "Bartleby"; the commitment to the
subject, the individuality and appreciativeness of the
writing, are admirable. What the story says, in general,
is that there is nothing good or bad but thinking makes
it so. The early pages display, comically, two contrasting
impressions of identical circumstances; nature's alphabet
is being read in two different moods. Not much writing in
English is more effectively hyperbolic than the successive
renderings of the cock's crow; these have a valid fullness
of effect. The crowing symbolises faith, glorifying daily
life and easing misery. First heard to the east, the cock

is not to be sold or given away, though its message can be shared. Not everybody hears it. The cock has been raised from the egg by Merrymusk, the woodman, himself; his ailing family find courage in it; it gives "stuff against despair"; it sounds like an angel in the Apocalypse; it "crows at the darkest; Glory to God in the highest!", "crowing the souls of the children out of their wasted bodies," dispelling the sting of death, the victory of the grave. But a moment after its last owner dies it dies too, and the narrator is left to crow on his own. Faith, one deduces, is a confidence-man whose counsels are effective as long as they are believed in; or perhaps Christianity, which once heartened men because taken as real, can now hearten only as a simulacrum. Belief works if one believes, and this tautology expresses the irony of the situation, since no reality need lie behind; faith can be solipsistic. "Cock-a-Doodle-Doo" is successfully ambiguous, cheerful in appearance, making a rueful grimace between the lines. Not bitter, though, as it has been thought—the feeling is richer than that, a glory in the subject, and a kind of glee in counterattacking a metaphysical puzzle. Behind the tale is the great dilemma: is faith (supposing it to be delusive) better than unfaith (supposing it to be true)?—the dilemma of Arnold's "Dover Beach," or Hardy's "Darkling Thrush," or *Clarel* itself. "Heartily wish Niebuhr & Strauss to the dogs," Melville was to comment in the 1856–7 *Journal*, "The deuce take their penetration & acumen. They have robbed us of the bloom. If they have undeceived any one —no thanks to them."[5]

"The Encantadas" stories amount to a Nature-poem, but not of a Wordsworthian kind. The Galapagos Islands seized Melville's imagination: in *Israel Potter* he compares the London crowds with the "convict tortoises" crawling over "vitreous rocks in the cursed Galapagos," and in "The Island" section of *Clarel* he expressed his haunted sense of their unearthly landscapes:

There clouds hang low, but yield no rain—
For ever hang, since wind is none
Or light; nor ship-boy's eye may gain
The smoke-wrapped peak, the inland one
Volcanic: this, within its shroud,
Streaked black and red, burns unrevealed;
It burns by night—by day the cloud
Shows leaden all, and dull and sealed.
The beach is cinders. With the tide
Salt creeks and ashy inlet bring
More loneness from the outer ring
Of ocean.[6]

More than superstitiously weird, they are physically and metaphysically weird also, signs that Nature can very well betray the heart that loves her. Melville drew on authorities, including Darwin (whose comparison of the islands to Wolverhampton iron-furnaces seems echoed in Melville's "dross of an iron-furnace"), but, far beyond anything he found, he treats the subject with his own realisation and a memorable energy. Such symbolism as there is does not work to the detriment of reality; "Two Sides to a Tortoise" earns its symbolical interpretation by the truth with which it conveys the animals' archaic and cumbersome endurance. The other best-known episode, that of the Chola Widow, is less concentrated and more touched with the South-Sea-sentimental, but it ends with a moving reticence which justifies the crucifixion theme.

As for "I and my Chimney," some readers have and others have not discovered in it figures-in-the-carpet. Melville's brother Allan, in annotating his copy, took it to be about nothing but Melville and his chimney, and Raymond Weaver quotes Colonel Lathers, a Pittsfield neighbour of Melville's, in praise of Melville's library, conversation, home-made cider, and capacious fireplace with the inscription, verified on windy days, "I and my Chimney smoke together." This, of course, has not ended the problem. The agitation, in the story, over the chimney, interpreters inform us, is the Melville family's concern for his sanity, or neurasthenia, or physique, or backbone (the bricks being vertebrae; one is virtually told what the particular breadth at its base refers to). Or it is Melville's struggle to preserve "his essential and deepest self,"[7] or "to live with his enormous and tantalising ego."[8] Something of this has to be recognised. There are overtones of a private gesture, a personal pun; the story has a resonance as a manifesto of Melville's sense of autonomy. Newton Arvin interprets its tone as "deep resentment." But such things are deducible only by an intent process of reading between the lines, and if "I and my Chimney" is not a cross between Lamb-like exuberance and a Yankee gift for exaggeration its real tone and manner must be more deeply disguised than is at all reasonable.

Some of the other tales are less interesting, though Melville sometimes gets an accentuation by antithetical pairing, as with "The Two Temples," "Poor Man's Pudding and Rich Man's Crumbs," "The Paradise of Bachelors," and "The Tartarus of Maids." "The Tartarus of Maids," though one critic has thought it to be a symbolisation of gestation so daring that Melville's readers would refrain from recognising it, seems to be what it purports to be, Melville's reaction to industrial misery, with the natural reflexion that the girls thus enslaved to the machine have lost the fertility of their lives. The sentiment was to reappear in *Clarel*:

> Old ballads sing
> Fair Christian children crucified
> By impious Jews; you've heard the thing:
> Yes, fable; but there's truth hard by:
> How many Hughs of Lincoln, say,
> Does Mammon in his mills today
> Crook, if he does not crucify?[9]

But the story best worth attention is "Benito Cereno."

The narrative is from Captain Amasa Delano's *Voyages and Travels* (1817).[10] Delano provides the facts, Melville the imagination. The images of forlornness and sinister lethargy, the dream-like equivocal inconsequence which foils the sensible Delano, the isolation, the leaden day, the current's drift, the ship's slow roll, are the perfect accompaniment, like Conrad's descriptions of the Golfo Placido in *Nostromo*. Detail is used realistically, but with a poetic imagination:

> Upon the tarnished head-boards, near by, appeared in stately capitals, once gilt, the ship's name, "SAN DOMINICK," each letter streakingly corroded with tricklings of copper-spike rust; while, like mourning weeds, dark festoons of sea-grass slimily swept to and fro over the name, with every hearse-like roll of the hull.[11]

Melville invents the oakum-pickers and axe-grinders as an ominous voiceless chorus, and also such details as the ship's forlorn picturesqueness, the skeleton, and Babo's murderous leap. These are natural embellishments. One other change, however, makes a radical difference. In Delano's account, Don Benito proves a monster of ingratitude and intrigue. In Melville's, he is a haunted, moody figure, spiritually destroyed by his experience of blackness, of "the negro" who has "cast such a shadow." In the imposition of its spell, in subtlety of detail, and in presentation of moral crisis, "Benito Cereno" can claim equivalence with Conrad's *Shadow Line*.

The *Journal of a Visit to Europe and the Levant, 1856–1857* evinces Melville's alert eye and intelligence. He had moods of depression, but the major effect is of vigorous response and interest. There is nothing flaccid in the description of a camel at Smyrna:

> From his long curved and crane-like neck, (which he carries stiffly like a clergyman in a stiff cravat) his feathery-looking forelegs, & his long lank hind ones,

he seems a cross between an ostrich & a gigantic grass-hopper. His hoof is spongy, & covered with hair to the ground, so that walking through these muddy lanes, he seems stilting along on four mops.[12]

(Still interested, Melville adds in the margins, "Carries his neck out like a tortoise. Tail like long eel, driver holds it & steers him. Has a way of turning his head so that his face & tail face you together.—A sort of saw-buck,—swaying of the rider.—height. Motion increases as in mast of ship. Camel seems built by nature with special precautions against man's use. The hump in way of saddle, but man outwits nature here.") Desolation of landscape and of spirit, as in the Galapagos, strikes him at the Dead Sea, yet his account is not without humour:

—foam on beach & pebbles like slaver of mad dog—smarting bitter of the water,—carried the bitter in my mouth all day—bitterness of life—thought of all bitter things—Bitter is it to be poor & bitter, to be reviled, & Oh bitter are these waters of Death, thought I.—Old boughs tossed up by water—relics of pick-nick—nought to eat but bitumen & ashes with des[s]ert of Sodom apples washed down with water of Dead Sea.[13]

At Patmos he feels "the great curse of modern travel—skepticism," and makes the remark on Niebuhr and Strauss already quoted. *Clarel*, the poetic record of this trip, twenty years later, was to comment that

> Zion, like Rome, is Niebuhrized:
> Yes, doubt attends. Doubt's heavy hand
> Is set against us.[14]

But the pessimism is touched with whimsical fancy, and Melville is not in that state of despondent nausea some biographers have assumed. In Rome he comments on antiquities and paintings most sensitively—"A Lady by Titian—the crimson & white sleeves. The golden haze of his pictures," "The remarkable Teniers effect is produced by first dwarfing, then deforming humanity," and, of Claude's canvases, "All their effect is of atmosphere. He paints the air." At Venice his eye is equally acute:

St: Mark's at sunset. gilt mosaics, pinnacles, looks like holyday affair. As if the Grand Turk had pitched his pavilion here for a summers day. 800 years! Inside the precious marbles, from extreme age, look like a mural of rare old soaps.—have an unctuous look. Fairly steamed with old devotions as refectories with old dinners.[15]

And the account of Oxford is most appreciative.[16]

The range and interest of these miscellaneous works is certainly not such as to suggest that after publishing one more novel Melville would fall silent. They are in a very different manner from *Moby Dick* and *Pierre* but still show every sign of addiction to the craft of writing and the pleasures of the imagination. The impetus may have lessened, and the imagination may be less ambitious. But the quality is still distinguished.

REFERENCES

1. *Complete Stories of Melville*, ed. J. Leyda, 1949, p. xxviii.
2. *Letters*, pp. 153–62.
3. *I.P.*, chs. xxiii–v.
4. Lewis Mumford, *Herman Melville*, p. 236.
5. *J. 1856*, p. 167.
6. *Clarel*, PT. IV, sect. iii (st. ed., II. 167).
7. Newton Arvin, *Herman Melville*, 1950, p. 205.
8. E. H. Rosenberry, *Melville and the Comic Spirit*, p. 181.
9. *Clarel*, PT. IV, sect. ix (st. ed., II. 192–3).
10. See H. H. Scudder, in *Publ. Mod. Lang. Assoc. Amer.*, XLIII (1928), pp. 502–32.
11. *Complete Stories of Melville*, ed. J. Leyda, p. 257.
12. *J. 1856*, p. 107.
13. *J. 1856*, p. 136.
14. *Clarel*, PT. I, sect. xxxiv (st. ed., I. 136).
15. *J. 1856*, pp. 234–5.
16. *J. 1856*, pp. 259–60.

CHAPTER VIII

THE CONFIDENCE-MAN

Before and after writing *The Confidence-Man* (1857), Melville was exercised by problems of trust and deception. In his Bible he marked "The workers of iniquity, which speak peace to their neighbours but mischief is in their hearts" (Ps. xxviii. 3); in his Homer he underlined "Blind Confidence, (The God of Fools)" (*Od.*, iii. 108); and in Emerson's *Essays*, against the sentiment "Trust men, and they will be true to you," he noted "God help the poor fellow who squares his life according to this." *Pierre* and "Benito Cereno" had dealt with ambiguous good and evil: "Cock-a-Doodle-Doo" had assumed that life needs faith—yet faith may have nothing behind it. *The Confidence-Man* faces a similar dilemma—the good life requires trust in God and man, yet God and man when trusted may deceive. The cynic guards himself, but is not humane; the humane man obeys his heart, but is duped. (More deservedly, the self-seeker is also duped, overreached by greater cunning, but naturally this does not distress one.) The *Pierre* problem is presented again, and Melville might have used as an epigraph Dryden's lines

> When I consider life, 'tis all a cheat;
> Yet, fool'd with hope, men favour the deceit.

The book has been very variously valued. "Of all his works the hardest nut to crack," the London *Critic* thought it (Apr. 1857); to the *Literary Gazette* it was "madness" (Apr. 1857). It is "a fog of undirected verbiage" to Van Wyck Brooks,[1] "a peak of his achievement" to Jay Leyda,[2] "an intellectual act of the greatest force and authority" to Richard Chase.[3] This last view

THE CONFIDENCE-MAN

is certainly too favourable, yet the book is interestingly novel (Melville was always experimenting), and its sharpness, shrewdness, and graphic quality contrast wholly with *Pierre*. It is true that its intentions are tricky, and its impersonations confusing; Melville, it seems, is delighting to try his readers' own gullibility; how much will they see through? That is only to say that the main mode is ironic, and much of the reader's pleasure comes from his necessary sharpening of attention. A masquerade of charlatans operating on April Fool's Day, the novel is an exercise in comprehensive outwitting.

Interpretations of its tone, as of its quality, have varied radically. The *Westminster Review* thought it "too much in the spirit of Timon" (Jul. 1857). Willard Thorp will not have the Timonism but thinks that Melville shows his actors "with a grim detachment that is more harrowing than a diatribe."[4] For Leon Howard, mankind is presented in a "cynical and melancholy" light.[5] Edward Rosenberry thinks the book Shandian, a matter of laughter throughout, and he suggests that Melville stopped writing novels not in Bartleby-like withdrawal but because he was tired of having his humour not appreciated.[6] Roy Fuller diagnoses "a little humour, much irony,"[7] and this is right enough, though indeed the quantity of humour is considerable. For some critics, the book moves steadily towards despair; for Leon Howard it starts as satire on gullibility but turns round in mid-course and becomes satire on faithlessness.[8] As for its contents, Richard Chase considers Melville to be viewing American society with "full clarity," making "his one definite adverse statement,"[9] while Yvor Winters, while judging the book important and impressive, yet thinks it "unsatisfactory as philosophy and tediously repetitious as narrative," written in "a kind of moral limbo." It has, he remarks, "left his critics in the most abysmal confusion."[10]

The first quotation the *Dictionary of American English*

gives for " Confidence-Man" is of 1849, but if the name
was new when Melville wrote the species was already
part of American folk-lore. The story is as much parable
as realism; Melville specifically claims the liberty of
occasional unrealism—"nature unfettered, exhilarated,
in effect transformed"—since a novel is to amuse, though
the result should be "more reality than real life itself can
show."[11] "An Anacharsis Clootz congress" of mankind[12]
(the same allusion as in *Moby Dick* and *Billy Budd*) is on a
trip like a Canterbury pilgrimage or a visit to Mecca; it
has, therefore, to do with the objects of faith. The ship,
Fidèle, carries all facilities for the public or private conduct of life. Passengers embark and disembark; this represents life's meetings and partings. The date is 1 April,
and to a wooden-legged misanthrope the travellers are a
"flock of fools, under this captain of fools, in this ship of
fools." A deaf-mute, of "aspect singularly innocent,"
"gentle and jaded," "in the extremest sense of the word,
a stranger," "somehow inappropriate to the time and
place," makes his "advent," and stands unrecognised
beside a placard warning travellers against an impostor
from the East; round this the crowd bustles inquisitively,
and pickpockets are at work. The stranger, presumably
himself the "impostor," holds up texts on charity from
1 Cor. XIII, which contrast with the "No Trust" sign of the
barber (the one who shaves you, presumably). But being
thought crazy he finds a "humble quarter," is soon forgotten, and disappears. He has come "from some far
country beyond the prairies" (eastwards, one assumes),
is "lamblike," and has "long been without the solace of
a bed." The Son of Man, we recall among other clues,
"hath not where to lay his head" (Mt. VIII. 20).

This, it would seem, signifies a silent, patient and self-
effacing deity, offering the supreme message of charity
to a world forewarned to reject it as alien; in his texts the
word Charity remains unobliterated, presumably as the
standing, essential element. The deaf-mute is a Christ-

like figure with St Paul's message, but silent either because Deity is silent or because no other part of Christian doctrine than charity remains valid. The sense is surely not that he is, as Richard Chase calls him, "a cruel, chimerical mask of Christ."[13] He is a contrasting form of the confidence-man's masquerade. The later confidence-men connect one with another in demonstrable sequence; each leaves as the next arrives, each knows of and vouches for his precursor or successor. The deaf-mute has no such relationship; ignored, humble, he makes no attempt to wheedle, and the appeal he bears to charity in no way resembles the "operators'" bland promulgation of *bonhomie*. He is, rather, an "impostor" to the codes of the world, a confidence-man (genuinely) for an undependable Heaven, appealing for divine trust in a world alien to it, a world which, whenever it recommends charity, does so to serve its own ends. The intention is presumably somewhat like that by which Mapple's sermon is placed early in *Moby Dick*, as a standard of reference, though now the faith of Christian love held up to the *Fidèle*'s passengers seems irrelevant to men's interests. As in *Clarel*, the world is

> a den
> Worse for Christ's coming, since His love
> (Perverted) did but venom prove.[14]

Perhaps in the early stages Melville meant to keep this Christian theme going. He has a good Episcopalian clergyman, "innocence, tenderness, and good sense triumvirate in his air,"[15] a vigorous Methodist, a generous merchant,[16] a charitable gentleman (though somewhat sardonically described), and a charitable lady.[17] The Methodist preaches trust, and does not seem a deceiver; presumably religion should inculcate faith even though the world denies it. The worldly passengers applaud him but take no heed; indeed, the Methodist himself is struck with doubts. Even the godly, it seems,

H

are not wholly prepared to apply trust on this earth. And who can blame them? *Pierre* had shown what ideal conduct in an unideal society can result in. Christian virtue, however, if present implicitly, and in parody-reminders, disappears generally from explicitness. Instead, "operators" get to work, some wholly deceiving, some partly self-deceived too. The first, a negro cripple, calls to one's mind the cheerful, deceit-masking subservience of Babo, the negro in "Benito Cereno." (It is hardly necessary to say that Melville's colour-convention is purely symbolical, not racial at all; in *Battle-Pieces* he writes of "the blacks, our fellow-men." The next few confidence-men have some degree of blackness about them in their dress; then the idea fades out.) Against a hostile one-legged misanthrope (if hypocrisy is lame, so is misanthropy) he names guarantors who will vouch for him, and they as they later appear in sequence refer back to him. He vanishes after slyly appropriating a good merchant's business card. From this, the next trickster, a man in mourning, has obviously learnt the details on which he claims the merchant's acquaintance and gulls him; he then in turn recommends the President of the Black Rapids Coal Company, John Truman. Before Truman appears, however, a man in grey, arriving as the mourner leaves, and leaving as Truman arrives, collects money for a bogus asylum. Truman keeps the sequence going by referring to his previous incarnations and recommending the next, a herb-doctor, who appears as Truman departs, and is succeeded by the agent of the Philosophical Intelligence Office and then by a euphoric cosmopolitan, who persists through the latter half of the book, meeting others like Winsome the Emersonian who are, in their own ways, confidence-men too. There are also anti-confidence-men, of varying degrees of gruffness, but even they are not invulnerable.

What, other than imposture, these characters represent is not clear. Nathalia Wright in *Melville's Use of the*

Bible offers an ingenious scheme by which, starting with the "advent" of the Christian ideal, the book presents bogus versions of the Beatitudes and the Pauline virtues; the negro is the poor in spirit, the mourner is those who mourn, the man in grey is the hungerer after righteousness, Truman with his ledger is Faith with the Bible, the herb-doctor is Hope, the Philosophical Intelligence agent is Charity, and the cosmopolitan is in appearance Christian brotherhood (though in fact expediency). Improbable though this all looks, the text bears it out tolerably well. But Melville's scheme allows more than one interpretation. The herb-doctor, for instance, is a Nature-benevolist in the Wordsworth-Emerson-Thoreau fashion; he brings to mind such of Thoreau's remarks as "Cold and damp—are they not as rich experience as warmth and dryness?" (*A Week on the Concord*), or "There was never yet such a storm but it was Aeolian music to a healthy and innocent ear" (*Walden*). The sceptical Missourian is clearly answering Thoreau when he objects, "Come, come, Mr Palaverer, for all your palavering, did you yourself never shut out nature of a cold wet night? . . . Whose hailstones smashed my windows?"[18] The Philosophical Intelligence agent, "cousin-german" of the herb-doctor, is a sort of optimistic humanist, philosophically convinced of human goodness as against the Missourian's St-Augustine-and-Original-Sin doctrine. The cosmopolitan "catholic man" Frank Goodman, "confidential clerk" of the diddlers as the Missourian thinks him, "ambassador from the human race," suggests specious philanthropy. At times he tries to touch his acquaintances for loans. He bilks the barber, briefly. Finally he takes charge of a white-haired old man reading his Bible under the one light remaining in the cabin. One assumes this to be traditional Old-and-New-Testament faith, its lamp still shining while "other lamps, barren planets," have gone out. The lamp, engraved with flaming altars (living faith?) and a haloed man

(Christ?), shines brightly on a marble table beneath it (clear, firm belief?) but more dimly into the corners. The old man sits gravely and courteously reading the book which a dozing passenger thinks "too good to be true." The cosmopolitan enters troubled by some pessimistic sentences from ecclesiasticus; these, both he and the old man are relieved to find, are merely in the Apocrypha, not part of accepted faith. Both settle again into serenity, but this is disturbed by a lad peddling travellers' safety-devices. Dressed in flame-coloured rags, with grimed face, and eyes sparkling "like lustrous sparks in fresh coal," he is, one guesses, a sort of diabolical imp. Unsettling the old believer, he sells his wares and goes, scraping a bow with "a hard foot" like a mischievous steer (the cloven hoof). The old man has lost that trust in the creature which is also trust in the Creator,[19] his Biblical faith has wilted, the lamp is dying, and the cosmopolitan shepherds him to bed somewhat consoled with a "very hollow" life-preserver in case of shipwreck. The cosmopolitan extinguishes the light, and the sacred signs go out; sociability has taken over the remnants of faith, in a world without supernatural light. T. S. Eliot's essay on *The Humanism of Irving Babbitt* is precisely relevant.

As with other books of Melville's, one uses most of one's critical space on exposition; with him, the critic is much more required than with most novelists to decide what the novels mean. This is a mixed blessing. On one hand, the necessary excogitation reveals many interlocking details, and heightens the sense of shrewd invention. On the other hand, one can get too tired of guessing which thimble the pea is under, or too eager to find peas under every thimble. The clues, moreover, are tricky. But if some of the meaning eludes one, each reading adds to the coherence; anyone prepared for, say, four readings will find that most of the pieces click, provided he reads in the light of Melville's earlier work also. He will have other satisfactions too, for the writing is intelligent and sharp (given some passages of confusion), moral qualities are rendered through graphic particulars and real speech-idiom, and there is much zest of description. There are pleasant essay-speculations, some striking witticisms, and the Emerson parody is brilliant.[20] Among the successes are the interspersed anecdotes which, unco-ordinated though they appear, are related to the episodic narrative by antithesis of tone and significance, and achieve an intensity, indeed a strangeness of overtone, that offsets the prevailing ironic but easy-going fantasy. The most remarkable is that of Moredock the Indian-hater, for it returns to the theme of the obsessed isolato. One thinks again of *Moby Dick*, for, as whalemen consider whales their destined prey, backwoodsmen, likewise the out-riders of society, are enemies to the Indians, being reared in a justified distrust of them. And as most whalers with whales, most backwoodsmen hate only in moderation, not with hatred as a passion in itself. But "the Indian hunter *par excellence* . . . makes a vow, the hate of which is a vortex from whose suction scarce the remotest chip of the guilty race may reasonably feel secure," and he seeks "implacable, lonesome vengeance." This is Moredock's case, suffering "signal outrage" in the murder of his mother and brothers, and devoting himself to destroying the enemy. These interspersed incidents have one impor-tant function; they face the optimistic confidence-mongers with the facts of treachery and of hatred. The Indians no more represent anti-Indian prejudice in Melville than the negro cripple represents anti-negro prejudice (or *Moby Dick* anti-whale prejudice); they symbolise the hostility men feel in Fate, and Moredock's passion is a late version of Ahab's hatred of "all that most maddens and torments." It suggests that Melville cherished at least a residual emotion of resentment against a universe now intellectually considered neutral and silent.

The Confidence-Man can be made out, though misleadingly, as tragically bitter in implication. Morally, it speaks for the charity the world denies; metaphysically, it recognises inscrutability, as does the poem "The Conflict of Convictions," in *Battle-Pieces*:

> Yea and Nay—
> Each hath his say;
> But God He keeps the middle way.
> None was by
> When he spread the sky;
> Wisdom is vain, and prophecy.

Certainly these themes are present, and centrally. But they are parts of such a miscellany that the total effect is less of gloom than of a shifting satiric fantasy of which the keynote is entertainment. Whatever the metaphysical implications, *The Confidence-Man* is, in its main effect, a comedy of folk-mythology, with bitterness underlying it, perhaps, but not so as to destroy its ironic gusto.

REFERENCES

1. Van Wyck Brooks, *Emerson and Others*, 1927, p. 177.
2. *Complete Stories of Melville*, ed. Jay Leyda, p. xxix.
3. Richard Chase, *Herman Melville*, p. 206.
4. *Herman Melville: Representative Selections*, ed. Willard Thorp, 1938, p. cxvi.
5. Leon Howard, *Herman Melville*, p. 228.
6. Edward H. Rosenberry, *Melville and the Comic Spirit*, pp. 146–8, 184.
7. *The Confidence Man*, Chiltern Library, 1948, p. x.
8. Leon Howard, *Herman Melville*, p. 237.
9. Richard Chase, *Herman Melville*, p. 185.
10. Yvor Winters, "Herman Melville," in *In Defense of Reason*, p. 229.
11. *C.M.*, ch. xxxiii.
12. *C.M.*, ch. ii.
13. Richard Chase, *Herman Melville*, pp. 187–8.
14. *Clarel*, PT. II, sect. xxi (st. ed., I. 254).
15. *C.M.*, ch. iii.
16. *C.M.*, *loc. cit.*
17. *C.M.*, chs. vii–viii.
18. *C.M.*, ch. xxi.
19. *C.M.*, ch. xlv.
20. *C.M.*, chs. xxxvi–vii.

CHAPTER IX

BILLY BUDD

Melville's last story is so lucid and thoughtful as to need little commentary; it is its own best expression of his mood in his last years, three decades and more after *The Confidence-Man*. We recognise again his lasting concerns— inscrutable Deity creating good and evil (yet here as in Shakespearian tragedy implicitly vindicating goodness); we recognise the mystery of wickedness previously presented in Jackson and Bland, and the problems of private conscience and the public code, and of heavenly justice and earthly ("Struck dead by an angel of God. Yet the angel must hang!"). And we recognise what the novels had long presented, the synoptic view through different temperaments. The subtitle is "An inside narration," and Melville communicates Claggart's sense of things, shrewd and hateful, Billy's guileless and shocked, and Vere's, grieved yet dutiful. Carefully the story advances from its early tones of manly comedy with the affectionate once-upon-a-time glamour of the Handsome Sailor, to the growing shades of evil, the sudden tragic act, the saddened courtmartial, and the ritual of execution to which Heaven gives the grace of apparent benediction. Melville imparts to the common life of man a certain ceremoniousness; no longer is it adrift, as in *Pierre*, or haphazard, as in *The Confidence-Man*. It is subject to accident, but the accident though morally shocking seems, as in Shakespearian tragedy, part of a mysterious inevitability. On the naval level, of course, the ceremoniousness is that of code and tradition; "with mankind," Vere remarks, "forms, measured forms, are everything; and that is the import couched in the story of Orpheus with his lyre, spell-binding the wild denizens of the wood." The story as a whole works likewise in "measured forms," changing the raw cruelty of life into the fated dignity of Greek drama. Tragedy happens when the fortifying traditional is cut across by the irrational. One thinks of Wordsworth's lines in *The Borderers*:

> Action is transitory,—a step, a blow,
> The motion of a muscle, this way or that—
> 'Tis done, and in the after-vacancy
> We wonder at ourselves, like men betrayed:
> Suffering is permanent, obscure, and dark,
> And shares the nature of infinity.

Yet this happens, as it were, within a parable-like order. So the tale, though sad, does not lacerate. Charity of spirit rises above personal anguish, and Billy's death, carried through without a sting, is a sacrifice of the good which somehow enhances goodness itself. One watches in hypnotised calm, steadied by prose gravely and almost hieratically dignified:

> The hull deliberately recovering from the periodic roll to leeward was just regaining an even keel, when the last signal a preconcerted dumb one was given. At the same moment it chanced that the vapory fleece hanging low in the East, was shot through with a soft glory as of the fleece of the Lamb of God seen in mystical vision and simultaneously therewith, watched by the wedged mass of upturned faces, Billy ascended; and, ascending, took the full rose of the dawn. In the pinioned figure, arrived at the yard-end, to the wonder of all no motion was apparent save that created by the ship's motion, in moderate weather so majestic in a great ship ponderously cannoned.

Distanced by retrospection the story gains in simplicity. The shipboard detail is ample but is not presented,

as in *White Jacket*, as an encyclopedia of naval life. The
crew is real, but only as choric participants, surrounding
the trio involved. Good and evil are to be observed in
human nature, for which the social context is merely a
frame, though a frame whose strong character provides
the precise governing conditions. Among the finest things
in Melville's work is the analysis of Claggart's mixed
yearning and malice, real in its strangeness, given without
the histrionics of Ahab. The analysis is probing, adum-
brative, quietly troubled, and more interesting than any
sensationalism could be. It presents, one might say,
original sin according to agnosticism. The technical
virtue of the moral enquiry is the degree to which it is
embodied in the story. Not that Melville avoids conduct-
ing his own discussion; there is a good deal of commentary.
But this all arises so fully from and so integrally in the
narrative that idea, character, and event belong together.
The morality is not a separable thing, and to import into
criticism discussions of fallen and unfallen man, for
instance, is to be too extraneous. One need not, as elsewhere, render the meaning down into terms other than
its own. The story beautifully unites, with moved acceptance of fate, Melville's best fictional world (men at sea),
his best manner (a rendering of life deeply sensed and
judged), his best wisdom (reverence for goodness in
trouble), and his best metaphysical interest (spiritual
power in its uncertain leaning to goodness). The best
things about it have been said by E. M. Forster in *Aspects
of the Novel*, relating the single story to Melville's whole
work so well as to be the most fitting end to this study:

Billy Budd is a remote unearthly episode, but it is a song
not without words, and should be read both for its own
beauty and as an introduction to more difficult works.
Evil is labelled and personified instead of slipping over
the ocean and round the world, and Melville's mind
can be observed more easily. What one notices in him

is that his apprehensions are free from personal worry, so that we become bigger not smaller after sharing them. . . . Melville—after the initial roughness of his realism—reaches straight back into the universal, to a blackness and sadness so transcending our own that they are indistinguishable from glory. He says, "In certain moods no man can weigh this world without throwing in something somehow like Original Sin to strike the uneven balance." He threw it in, that undefinable something, the balance righted itself, and he gave us harmony and temporary salvation.[1]

REFERENCE

1. E. M. Forster, *Aspects of the Novel*, 1927, p. 184.

BIBLIOGRAPHY

I. HERMAN MELVILLE

The Standard Edition of Melville's works is not easily available, and editions of separate works are very miscellaneous. References in the notes are therefore made, in general, merely to relevant chapters or sections of works, which can be traced in any edition. Melville's chapters and sections are nearly always short, and identification should not cause trouble. Supplementary references are, however, given to the Standard Edition by chapter, volume, and page, whenever a precise reference may be helpful. The two volumes of *Mardi* in the Standard Edition have separate chapter numbers for each volume (Vol. I, chs. i–civ; Vol. II, chs. i–xci). The two volumes of *Moby Dick* in the Standard Edition have continuous chapter numbers, but, following the original American edition, an extra chapter is printed after ch. xxiv. Subsequent chapter numbers are therefore one greater in the Standard Edition and American editions than in most English editions. The note references to *Moby Dick* make clear this difference by indicating both series of numberings. References to *Pierre* are given to the books and sections into which all editions of this work are divided. References to the letters are to the Yale Edition [2, below].

1. Individual Works

These are arranged in order of composition, not necessarily in order of publication. The first published edition is mentioned, together with some useful later editions; these, however, are not listed exhaustively.

"Fragments from a Writing Desk." New York (Lansingburgh) 1839.
Typee: A Peep at Polynesian Life During a Four Months' Residence in a Valley of the Marquesas. London and New York 1846. The earliest edn., published in London, was entitled *Narrative of a Four Months' Residence among the Natives of a Valley of the Marquesas Islands: A Peep at Polynesian Life.* Also: (*i*), ed. W. Clark Russell, London (John Lane) and New York 1904; (*ii*), World's Classics, London 1924; (*iii*), ed. Robert Gibbings, Folio Society, London 1951; (*iv*), ed. Milton M. Stern, Everyman's Library, London and New York 1955; and many more.
Review of J. R. Browne, *Etchings of a Whaling Cruise.* New York 1847.
Omoo. New York and London 1847. Also: (*i*), ed. W. Clark Russell, London (John Lane) and New York 1904; (*ii*), World's Classics, London 1924; (*iii*), Evergreen Books, New York (Grove Press) and London (Calder) 1958; and many more.
Authentic Anecdotes of "Old Zack." New York 1847.

Mardi: And a Voyage Thither. London and New York 1849. Also: Abbey Classics, London (Chapman and Dodd) 1923.

Redburn: His First Voyage. New York and London 1849. Also: (*i*), Miscellany Series, London (Constable) 1929; (*ii*), ed. William Plomer, London (Cape) 1937; (*iii*), Anchor Books, New York (Doubleday) 1958; and many others.

White Jacket: or The World in a Man-of-War. New York and London 1850. Also: (*i*), ed. Carl van Doren, World's Classics, London 1924; (*ii*), ed. William Plomer, Chiltern Library, London (John Lehmann) 1952; (*iii*), Evergreen Books, New York (Grove Press) and London (Calder) 1956; and others.

Journal of a Visit to London and the Continent by Herman Melville, 1849–1850. Ed. Eleanor Melville Metcalf. Cambridge, Mass., 1948 and London (Cohen and West) 1949.

"A Thought on Book-binding." New York 1850.

"Hawthorne and his *Mosses*." New York 1850. Also in *The Shock of Recognition*, ed. Edmund Wilson, New York 1942.

Moby Dick. London and New York 1851. The earliest edn., published in London, was entitled *The Whale*. Also (*i*), ed. Viola Meynell, World's Classics, London 1920; (*ii*), ed. Raymond M. Weaver, New York (A. & C. Boni) 1925; (*iii*), New York (Random House) 1945; (*iv*), ed. Montgomery Belgion, London (Cresset Press) 1947; (*v*), ed. Willard Thorp, New York (Oxford U.P.) 1947; (*vi*), ed. Newton Arvin, New York 1948; (*vii*), ed. W. Somerset Maugham, Philadelphia (J. C. Winston) 1949; (*viii*), ed. Leon Howard, Modern Library, New York 1950; (*ix*), edd. L. S. Mansfield and H. P. Vincent, New York (Hendricks House) 1952; (*x*), ed. Sherman Paul, Everyman's Library, London and New York 1954; (*xi*), ed. Alfred Kazin, Boston (Houghton Mifflin) 1956 (Mr Kazin's intro. is reprinted in *American Critical Essays; Twentieth Century*, ed. H. Beaver, World's Classics, London 1959) ; and many more.

Pierre: or, the Ambiguities. New York 1852. Also: (*i*), ed. R. S. Forsyth, New York (Knopf) 1930; (*ii*), ed. H. A. Murray, New York (Hendricks House) 1949; (*iii*), Evergreen Books, New York (Grove Press) and London (Calder) 1958.

"Bartleby, the Scrivener." New York 1853.

"Cock-a-Doodle-Doo." New York 1853.

"The Encantadas." New York 1854. Also: ed. Victor Wolfgang von Hagen, Burlingame, Calif., 1940.

"The Two Temples." Written 1854; first pub. London 1924.

"Poor Man's Pudding and Rich Man's Crumbs." New York 1854.

"The Happy Failure." New York 1854.

"The Lightning-rod Man." New York 1854.

Israel Potter: his Fifty Years of Exile. New York 1854–5. Also: (*i*), ed.

Raymond M. Weaver, New York (A. & C. Boni) and London (Jarrold) 1924; (*ii*), ed. Lewis Leary, Sagamore 1957.

"The Paradise of Bachelors and Tartarus of Maids." New York 1855.

"The Bell-Tower." New York 1855.

"Jimmy Rose." New York, 1855.

"Benito Cereno." New York 1855.

"I and my Chimney." New York 1856.

"The 'Gees." New York 1856.

The Piazza Tales. New York 1856. Also: ed. Egbert S. Oliver, New York (Hendricks House) 1948.

"The Apple-tree Table." New York 1856.

Journal up the Straits, October 11, 1856–May 5, 1857. Ed. R. M. Weaver, New York 1935. For serious study, the next item is preferable.

Journal of a Visit to Europe and the Levant, October 11, 1856–May 6, 1857. Ed. Howard C. Horsford, Princeton 1955.

The Confidence-Man, his Masquerade. New York 1857. Also: (*i*), ed. Roy Fuller, Chiltern Library, London (John Lehmann) 1948; (*ii*), ed. Elizabeth S. Foster, New York (Hendricks House) 1954; and (*iii*), Evergreen Books, New York (Grove Press) and London (Calder) 1955.

Battle-Pieces and Aspects of the War. New York 1866. Also: ed. S. Kaplan, facsimile, Gainsville, Florida, 1960.

Clarel: A Poem and Pilgrimage in the Holy Land. New York 1876. Also: ed. Walter E. Bezanson, New York (Hendricks House) 1960.

John Marr and Other Sailors. New York 1888.

Timoleon. New York 1891.

"Daniel Orme." Written *c.* 1888–91; first pub. London 1924.

"Baby Budd, Sailor." Written *c.* 1888; first pub. Cambridge, Mass., 1948. See next item.

Billy Budd. Written 1888–91; first pub. 1924. *Melville's Billy Budd,* ed. F. Barron Freeman, Cambridge, Mass., 1948, which contains the definitive version, with a valuable intro. and the first publication of "Baby Budd, Sailor," is indispensable for serious study. Also: (*i*), ed. Rex Warner, Chiltern Library, London (John Lehmann) 1951; (*ii*), with *Typee*, ed. Milton B. Stern, Everyman's Library, London and New York 1958.

2. *Complete Collections*

The Works of Herman Melville. Standard Edition, 16 vols., London (Constable) 1922–4. Contents: I, *Typee;* II, *Omoo*; III–IV, *Mardi*; V, *Redburn*; VI, *White Jacket*; VII–VIII, *Moby Dick*; IX, *Pierre*; X, *Piazza Tales*; XI, *Israel Potter*; XII, *The Confidence-Man*; XIII, *Billy Budd and other Prose Pieces*; XIV–XV, *Clarel*; XVI, *Poems* (*Battle-Pieces, John Marr and other Poems, Timoleon &c.*).

Collected Poems of Herman Melville, ed. Howard P. Vincent, Chicago (Packard) and New York (Hendricks House) 1947.
The Letters of Herman Melville, ed. Merrell R. Davis and William H. Gilman, New Haven 1960.

3. Incomplete Collections and Series, and Selections

The St Botolph Library of Unusual Fiction, Boston 1923–5, contains: *Mardi, Redburn, White Jacket,* and *Israel Potter.*

The Library Edition, London (Cape) 1924, contains: *Typee, Omoo, Mardi, Redburn, White Jacket, Moby Dick,* and *Israel Potter.*

An edition in progress, New York (Hendricks House), contains: *Collected Poems,* ed. Howard P. Vincent, 1947; *Piazza Tales,* ed. Egbert S. Oliver 1948; *Pierre,* ed. Henry A. Murray 1949; *Moby Dick,* edd. Luther S. Mansfield and Howard P. Vincent, 1952; *The Confidence-Man,* ed. Elizabeth S. Foster, 1954; and *Clarel,* ed. Walter E. Bezanson, 1960.

Redburn, Moby Dick, Shorter Novels, and a *Portable Melville* are published by Mayflower Books.

Omoo, White Jacket, Pierre, and *The Confidence-Man* are in Evergreen Books, New York (Grove Press) and London (Calder).

The Apple-tree Table, and other Sketches, ed. H. Chapin, Princeton 1922, contains: "The Apple-tree Table"; "Hawthorne and his Mosses"; "Jimmy Rose"; "I and my Chimney"; "The Paradise of Bachelors and the Tartarus of Maids"; "Cock-a-Doodle-Doo"; "The Fiddler" [prob. not Melville]; "Poor Man's Pudding and Rich Man's Crumbs"; "The Happy Failure"; "The 'Gees."

John Marr and Other Poems, ed. H. Chapin, Princeton 1922, contains poems from the *John Marr* volume, *Battle-Pieces, Timoleon, Mardi,* and *Clarel,* and the prose "Supplement" to *Battle-Pieces.*

Shorter Novels, ed. R. M. Weaver, New York 1928, contains: "Benito Cereno," "Bartleby," "The Encantadas," and *Billy Budd.*

The Romances of Herman Melville, New York (Tudor) 1931, contains: *Typee, Omoo, Mardi, Moby Dick, White Jacket, Israel Potter,* and *Redburn.*

Herman Melville: Representative Selections, ed. (with intro., bibliography and notes) Willard Thorp, American Writers series, New York 1938, has a valuable intro., and (up to its date) a good bibliography, and contains selections from: *Typee, Omoo, Mardi, White Jacket, Moby Dick,* and the criticism, poems, and letters.

Selected Tales and Poems, ed. Richard Chase, New York 1950.

The Complete Stories of Herman Melville, ed. (with intro. and notes) Jay Leyda, New York (Random House) 1949 and London (Eyre & Spottiswoode) 1951.

Selected Writings of Herman Melville, New York (Random House) 1952, is a reprint of *The Complete Stories of Herman Melville*, without the editorial material, but with *Typee* and *Billy Budd*.

Melville as Lecturer, by Merton M. Sealts, jr, Cambridge, Mass., 1957, as far as possible assembles Melville's lectures.

II. OTHERS

ANDERSON, CHARLES R.: *Melville in the South Seas*, New York 1939.

—— (ed.): *Journal of a Cruise to the Pacific Ocean, 1842–4, in the frigate 'United States'*, Durham, North Carolina 1937.

ARVIN, NEWTON: *Herman Melville*, London 1950.

AUDEN, W. H.: *The Enchaféd Flood*, London 1951.

BEWLEY, MARIUS: *The Eccentric Design*, New York and London 1959.

BEZANSON, WALTER E.: "*Moby-Dick*: Work of Art"; see below, HILLWAY and MANSFIELD, *Moby-Dick: Centennial Essays*.

BLACKMUR, R. P.: "The Craft of Herman Melville," in *The Lion and the Honeycomb*, New York and London 1956.

BRASWELL, WILLIAM: *Melville's Religious Thought*, Durham, North Carolina 1943.

BROOKS, VAN WYCK: *Emerson and Others*, London 1927.

——: *The Flowering of New England*, New York 1936.

——: *The World of Washington Irving*, New York 1944.

——: *The Times of Melville and Whitman*, New York 1947.

CHASE, RICHARD: *Herman Melville: a Critical Study*, New York 1949.

CURL, VEGA: *Pasteboard Masks*, Cambridge, Mass., 1931.

DAMON, S. FOSTER: "Pierre the Ambiguous," in *Hound and Horn*, VOL. II, pp. 107–18, Camden, New Jersey, 1929.

DAVIS, MERRELL R.: "Flower Symbolism in *Mardi*," in *Modern Language Quarterly*, II (1941), pp. 625–38, Seattle.

——: *Melville's Mardi: a Chartless Voyage*, New Haven 1952.

DUYCKINCK, EVERT A. and GEORGE L. (edd.): *Cyclopædia of American Literature*, VOL. II, New York 1855.

FORSTER, E. M.: *Aspects of the Novel*, London 1927.

FREEMAN, F. BARRON: *Melville's Billy Budd*, Cambridge, Mass., 1948.

FREEMAN, JOHN: *Herman Melville*, London 1926.

GEIST, STANLEY: *Herman Melville: the Tragic Vision and the Heroic Ideal*, Cambridge, Mass., 1939.

GILMAN, W. H.: *Melville's Early Life and "Redburn,"* New York 1951.

HETHERINGTON, HUGH W.: "Early Reviews of *Moby-Dick*"; see below, HILLWAY and MANSFIELD, *Moby-Dick: Centennial Essays*.

HILLWAY, TYRUS: "A Preface to *Moby-Dick*"; see below, HILLWAY and MANSFIELD, *Moby-Dick: Centennial Essays*.

HILLWAY, TYRUS, and LUTHER S. MANSFIELD (edd.): *Moby-Dick: Centennial Essays*, Dallas 1953. Particularly useful items are listed under BEZANSON, HETHERINGTON, HILLWAY, and MILLER.

HOWARD, LEON: *Herman Melville*, Berkeley 1951.

KAZIN, ALFRED: "Ishmael and Ahab," in *American Critical Essays: Twentieth Century*, ed. H. Beaver, World's Classics, London 1959.

LAWRENCE, D. H.: *Studies in Classic American Literature*, London 1924.

LEVIN, HARRY: *The Power of Blackness*, New York 1958.

LEYDA, JAY: *The Melville Log*, 2 vols., New York 1951.

MASON, RONALD: *The Spirit Above the Dust*, London 1951.

MATTHIESSEN, F. O.: *American Renaissance*, New York 1941.

MAYOUX, JEAN JACQUES: *Melville*, tr. John Ashbery, New York and London 1960.

METCALF, ELEANOR MELVILLE: *Herman Melville: Cycle and Epicycle*, Cambridge, Mass., 1953.

MILLER, PERRY: "Melville and Transcendentalism;" see above, HILLWAY and MANSFIELD, *Moby-Dick: Centennial Essays*.

——: *The Raven and the Whale*, New York 1956.

MUMFORD, LEWIS: *Herman Melville*, New York and London 1929.

PARKES, H. B.: *The American Experience*, New York 1947.

PERCIVAL, M. O.: *A Reading of "Moby-Dick,"* Chicago 1950.

PURCELL, JAMES M.: "Melville's Contribution to English," in *Publ. Mod. Lang. Assoc. Amer.*, LVI (1941), pp. 797–808.

ROSENBERRY, E. H.: *Melville and the Comic Spirit*, Cambridge, Mass., 1955.

SCUDDER, H. H.: "Benito Cereno and Captain Delano," in *Publ. Mod. Lang. Assoc. Amer.*, XLIII (1928), pp. 502–32.

SEALTS, MERTON M.: *Melville as Lecturer*, Cambridge, Mass., 1957.

SEDGWICK, W. E.: *Herman Melville: The Tragedy of Mind*, Cambridge, Mass., 1945.

THOMPSON, LAWRANCE R.: *Melville's Quarrel with God*, Princeton 1952.

THORP, WILLARD: "Redburn's Prosy Old Guide Book," in *Publ. Mod. Lang. Assoc. Amer.*, LIII (1938), pp. 1146–56.

——: *Herman Melville: Representative Selections*, New York 1938.

VINCENT, HOWARD P.: *The Trying-Out of "Moby-Dick,"* Boston, Mass., 1949.

WATTERS, R. E.: "Melville's Isolatoes," in *Publications of the Modern Language Association of America*, LX (1945), pp. 1138–48.

WEAVER, RAYMOND M.: *Herman Melville: Mariner and Mystic*, New York 1921.

WINTERS, YVOR: "Herman Melville and the Problems of Moral Navigation," in *Maule's Curse*, New York 1938; also in *In Defense of Reason*, Denver 1947.

WRIGHT, NATHALIA: *Melville's Use of the Bible*, Durham, North Carolina 1949.